CW00538366

DL

ISLE OF WIGHT MOTOR VEHICLES 1896–1939

Chine Publishing

Mark Chessell

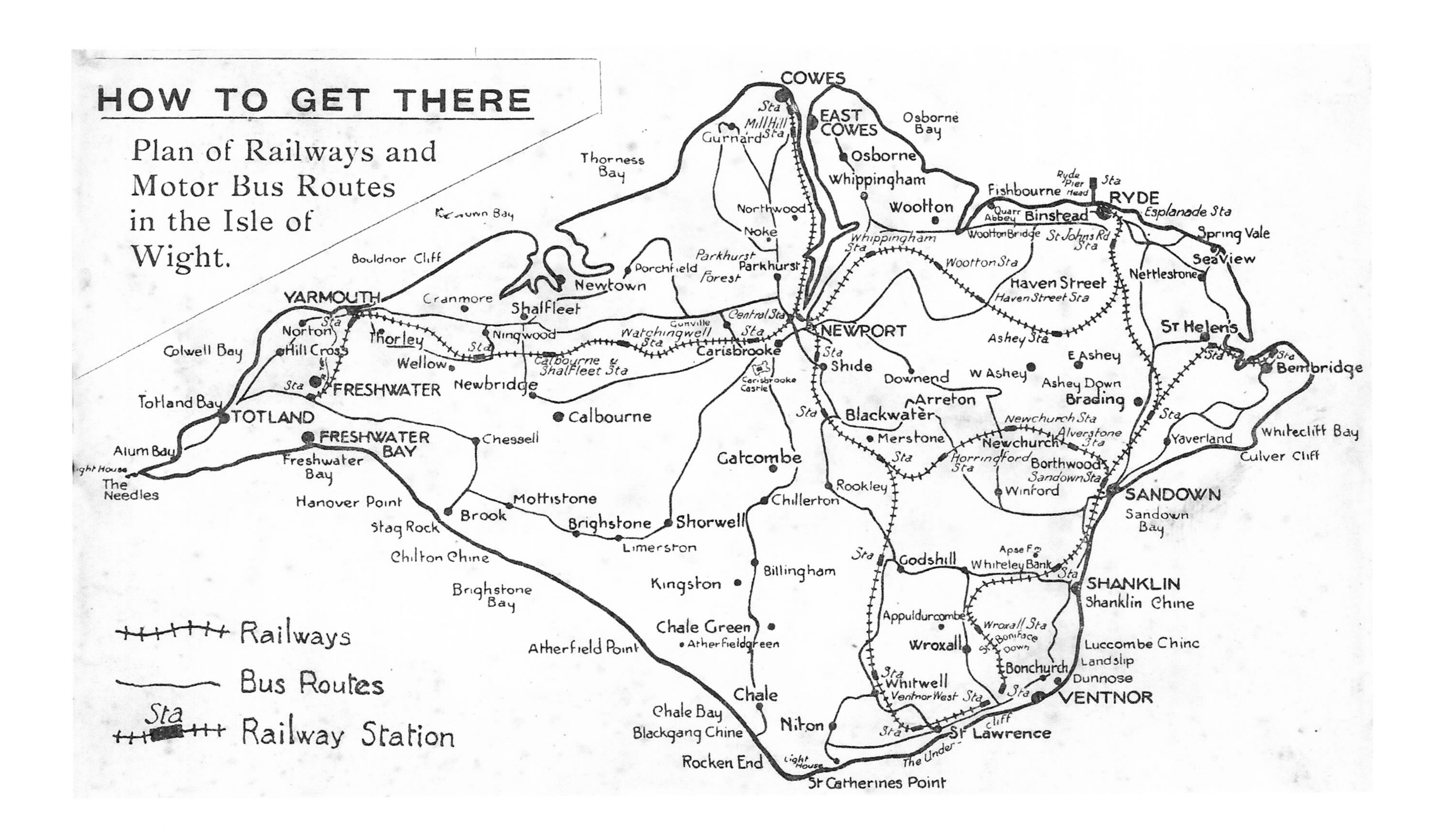

First published 2014
Published by: Chine Publishing
www.chinepublishing.co.uk

Printed by Parksons Graphics
ISBN: 978-0-9573692-1-4
Copyright: Mark Chessell

Cover photo: One of the earliest DL-registered cars was DL 85, a handsome Humber manufactured in Coventry c.1905.

Back cover: This photograph, taken by the author in November 2013, shows five superb vintage Isle of Wight motor vehicles. They have all been restored by Bob Stay and form part of his private collection.

CONTENTS

INTRODUCTION AND ACKNOWLEDGEMENTS

The identity of the Isle of Wight is made up of a number of key components. First and foremost there is the Island's remarkably varied geology, landscape and coast with around 50% being designated as an Area of Outstanding Natural Beauty or Heritage Coast. Carisbrooke Castle, Osborne House, Shanklin Chine, Alum Bay's coloured sands, the Needles, Parkhurst prison, Ryde pier, thatched cottages, dinosaur fossils and red squirrels are some of the Island's most distinctive and famous places and features. In addition there are several nationally important annual events – notably Cowes regatta, the music festivals and the garlic festival – plus some colourful local carnivals. Queen Victoria loved spending time on the Isle of Wight and this special 'microcosm of England' has provided creative inspiration for many poets, artists, writers and photographers. Islanders are renowned for their independence, determination, inventiveness and community spirit. For many years tourism has been very important within a diverse yet fragile local economy.

On the transport front the Isle of Wight is well known for its cross-Solent car and passenger ferries including the world's longest established hovercraft service from Southsea to Ryde and the chain ferry across the mouth of the river Medina from West Cowes to East Cowes. Up to the mid-1960s there was an extensive network of rural branch railways operated by steam trains. The main bus operator since 1929 has been Southern Vectis. Ships, yachts, light aircraft, hovercraft and various motor vehicles have been designed and manufactured locally by enterprising businesses and skilled workers within the cutting-edge engineering sector.

For virtually all of the twentieth century another important part of the Isle of Wight's identity was the characteristic 'DL' number plates carried by local motor vehicles. Many of these are still to be seen in use on the Island and mainland, with some displayed as personalised or cherished plates on newer vehicles. They are becoming less and less common, however, following their replacement by 'HW' numbers for new vehicles from September 2001 onwards.

As a child in the 1950s my late parents Don and Eileen Chessell introduced a travel game for my brother and myself to look out for DL-registered vehicles which came from the Isle of Wight. Fifty years on I still find myself noticing DL number plates whether they are on the road from Cowes to Newport or travelling around London on the M25!

Over the past few years I have collected and taken many photographs of older DL-registered vehicles. Detailed official records of the 14,000 or so vehicles registered in Newport up to 1939 have been very hard to obtain, especially for the period up to 1926. Despite the research difficulties, however, I hope that this coffee table book will provide an informative and entertaining journey into this aspect of the Isle of Wight's local history.

The book contains a representative selection of images of cars, motorcycles, buses, charabancs, coaches, taxis, commercial vehicles and traction engines that served local businesses, families and communities up to the start of the Second World War. I have sought to include pictures that feature people as well as vehicles and have supplied names of individuals, locations and dates where known. These photographs provide a fascinating glimpse of the wide range of early motor vehicles on the Isle of Wight. Most of the period images are black and white photographs, very few of which have been published before. Wherever possible I have sought to obtain the permission of photographers and copyright holders to include their excellent pictures.

There are also many colour photographs of pre-war vehicles. Incredibly, more than a hundred of these have survived well into the current century with their original Isle of Wight registration numbers. Some of the pictures of beautifully restored vintage vehicles have been taken by the author specifically for the 'survivors' chapter.

I wish to express my sincere gratitude to many organisations and people who have shown me their preserved pre-war DL-registered vehicles, lent photographs, identified vehicles, shared relevant information (including some memories of the Island before 1939) or commented on draft versions. In particular I would like to thank Carisbrooke Castle Museum, the Isle of Wight Council Museum, the Isle of Wight County Club, the Isle of Wight County Press, the Isle of Wight Record Office, Ventnor and District Local History Society, the Veteran Car Club of Great Britain, the late Fay Brown, Anna Buckett, Jeremy Chessell, Alan Cross, George Davis, Marilyn Earley, Mark Earp, Norman Fallick, Richard Flack, Keir Foss, John Golding, Geoff Golding, Bryan Goodman, John Gregory, David Hales, Patrick Hall, Tim Harding, Robert E. Jowitt, Alan Milbank, Geoff Morris, John Nash, Barry Price, Peter Relf, Tim Sargeant, Bob Stay, Colin Thomas, Don Vincent and John Wagstaff.

In addition I am extremely grateful to Jim Whiting of Capital Transport Publishing for his first class professional advice and direct input. I would also like to put on record my appreciation of the superb technical expertise of my nephew Sam Chessell. Sam has been able to restore over twenty fragile, faded or damaged 'DL' images to their former glory. Finally I wish to express my biggest thanks to my wife Susan who has provided insightful and steadfast support and encouragement during the past two years as I have brought this challenging project to fruition.

Throughout my research I have tried very hard to ensure that the information is as accurate as possible but it is almost inevitable that the book may contain a few errors. I should be pleased if any reader will contact me through the Chine Publishing email address (info@chinepublishing.co.uk) if they do identify any inaccuracies or omissions.

Sutton, Surrey, October 2014 Mark Chessell MRTPI CMILT

1 PRE-DL MOTOR VEHICLES

The dawn of motorised transport on the Isle of Wight took place in the final few years of Queen Victoria's reign and the early part of the Edwardian period. There had been some steam-powered stationary agricultural engines and traction engines in use in the late nineteenth century. However it was not until the Locomotives on Highways Act, 1896 was passed that motor vehicles began to appear on the roads of England in significant numbers. This piece of legislation removed the long-established requirement for a pedestrian to carry a red flag in front of a mechanically powered road vehicle. The Act provided a stimulus for the development and use of steam-powered and motorised road vehicles which had been held back for many years by the political influence of the manufacturers and owners of horse-drawn vehicles and powerful railway companies.

Initially there was no official vehicle registration system throughout the country and cars did not carry number plates. Prior to registration numbers, several owners took to 'naming' their cars, some even sporting special cast plates. One such car was Oliver Stanton's large Daimler known as 'Le Chat Noir'; another was an early 7hp Panhard known as 'Le Papillon Bleu'. This latter vehicle survives.

As the number of mechanically powered vehicles increased and accidents and motoring offences started to occur it was clear that a means of identifying individual cars was needed. One of the main provisions of the Motor Car Act of 1903 (which replaced the Locomotives on Highways Act of 1896) was that from 1st January 1904 every motor vehicle was required to be registered with a unique number plate. A national system of area codes for counties and county boroughs was introduced and the code 'DL' was allotted to the Isle of Wight. From this date the Isle of Wight County Council was authorised to issue individual registration numbers for the existing unregistered and all newly manufactured local motor vehicles. This initial registration system provided the capacity for issuing almost 10,000 unique number plates to Isle

of Wight vehicles (i.e. DL 1 to DL 9999). These numbers were expected to meet local needs for many years. Another important feature of the Act was that the standard speed limit was raised for the whole country to 20m.p.h.

Records of the pre-DL motor vehicles are very limited. A few photographs and postcards of very early cars without number plates do exist but details of vehicle types and ownership are almost non-existent.

One notable exception relates to the steam powered road vehicles which were produced by the Liquid Fuel Engineering Company (LIFU) at East Cowes from 1896 to 1900. This firm, which had been established by the American inventor Henry House, originally focused on the manufacture of steam powered launches for wealthy yacht owners. House recognised the emerging opportunities for the rapid development of steam powered road transport. Subsequently LIFU diversified its business to produce a range of vehicles (vans, open lorries, cars and charabancs) which were based on a standard chassis and which were assembled in an efficient manner by approximately 220 skilled workers.

In the late 1890s there was a great deal of experimentation taking place with new mechanically-propelled road vehicles. There was intense competition between steam-powered and motor vehicles for around ten years until the internal combustion engine proved itself as the most reliable driving force for most vehicles. The main exception to this situation was the transport of heavy goods. Steam-powered lorries and vans were capable of hauling much heavier loads than early motorised commercial vehicles. Indeed some firms (e.g. Sentinel and Foden) continued to manufacture such vehicles up to the 1930s.

During the early years of steam-powered road vehicle production LIFU was one of the leading manufacturers in England. Their patented vehicles had paraffin-fired boilers fitted under the bonnet and this gave them major economic and operational advantages over conventional coal-fuelled vehicles. The photograph on page 5 shows one of LIFU's earliest production models, dating from around 1897.

In May 1898 a national competition was held in Liverpool to compare the performance of various steam-powered lorries. Four vehicles (two Thornycrofts, one Leyland and a LIFU) entered the main class of the contest which involved carrying a two ton load over a 35 mile circuit on normal roads on four consecutive days. The lorries were set off at timed intervals and it is noteworthy that the LIFU vehicle completed the course and recorded the fastest time on each day, significantly outperforming its three rivals. For its best run the LIFU vehicle recorded a time of 4 hours and 9 minutes, an average speed of almost 9m.p.h.

The type of LIFU vehicle which took part in the Liverpool trials is illustrated on page 6 in this drawing by Don Vincent. LIFU road-tested their new vehicles in and around East Cowes and several complaints were made by local residents about the speed that Mr Henry House junior was driving at during such tests. In January 1899 the police set up a 'speed trap'. Mr House was later found guilty of travelling at more than 18m.p.h. (more than twice the speed limit at that time) and fined three pounds with eleven shillings costs.

By 1898 LIFU was manufacturing steam-powered open lorries, enclosed vans, cars and charabancs. Most vehicles were built on a standard chassis with the bodywork being provided to meet the specification of the customer. In 1899 thirty road vehicles were made with every part being manufactured in the Columbine yard, which later became the site of the famous Saunders-Roe factory. Between 1899 and 1900 the accomplished coachbuilder R. Bird Cheverton of Newport was responsible for trimming the LIFU vehicle bodies and for making and binding the wheels. Unfortunately, following the death of the financier R.R. Symon, LIFU was forced to leave its East Cowes factory and all the stock and machinery was sold. The company continued to produce a small number of steam-powered cars on the mainland for a few years but failed to fulfil its early promise as a successful manufacturer.

The only known surviving LIFU road vehicle is shown in the photo on page 9, which was taken around 1950. This historic steam-powered car was built around 1901 by T Noakes and Son, London under contract to Henry Alonso House (of Poole). It is currently on display at the Ironbridge Museum in the West Midlands. The vehicle was kept at the National Motor Museum at Beaulieu for many years and has taken part in several Veteran

Examples of some early LIFU passenger vehicles produced at East Cowes between 1896 and 1900

Car Club of Great Britain events. Although this vehicle was built on the mainland much of the design and development work for this more advanced model probably took place at East Cowes.

In the May 18th 1901 issue of 'the Autocar' it was reported that at 5pm on the last day of the Automobile Club Exhibition the new light LIFU car ran into the arena, completing a most successful run of 110 miles from Poole, Dorset, whence she was driven by Mr H A House. This was her first trip upon the road and she ran scentlessly and noiselessly in the arena. The steam car weighed 14cwt and was driven by a horizontal ten nominal horse-power two-cylinder compound engine. The body fitted was commodious and roomy, and accommodated four most comfortably. Artillery wheels with solid tyres were fitted. Colonel Crompton, R.E., expressed himself as most satisfied with the vehicle's turnout

and behaviour and said that he had already notched her down for submission to the War Office Mechanical Transport Committee. Sadly, it would appear that very few examples of this promising English-built steam car were ever produced.

The three-wheeled vehicle pictured on the left is an 'English Mechanic' car, built by blacksmith Arthur Creeth in Nettlestone around 1903. The English Mechanic was a regular journal for early motorists and it supplied instructions for keen mechanical engineers to build their own vehicle, month by month. It is not known how many of these cars were built but it is believed that relatively few of them were assembled successfully. Engineers could choose to build three or four wheeled cars powered by internal combustion or steam engines. Arthur Creeth's workshop-built steam-powered car was a major pioneering achievement. According to Creeth family records Arthur drove this open two seat vehicle between Nettlestone and Brighstone (a distance of about fifteen miles) a number of times.

A second example of a pre-registration Isle of Wight car is shown in the postcard view of Cowes Parade, c.1903 on page 10. This shows a Clement car with its two occupants enjoying the view over the Solent.

The above photograph shows a Christmas card which was sent to two Ventnor residents. The image was donated to the Ventnor and District Local History Society. It shows a 1902 De Dion Bouton Model K 8hp tonneau. Unfortunately it is not known whether the owner of this pre-registration vehicle lived on the Island.

2 DL VEHICLES 1904 to 1918

In December 1903 the Isle of Wight County Council's Motor Vehicle Licensing Office began issuing DL number plates to all motor vehicles registered on the Island. Initially this involved allocating the earliest numbers (up to around DL 50) to existing vehicles which had been built in the late 1890s and early 1900s and owned by Islanders. Details of individual registration numbers, the names of the original owners and their town or village were recorded in an official register. Volume 1 covered the period up to October 1926 and contained information on almost 5000 registrations (DL 1 to DL 4900). Unfortunately it has not been possible to trace the location of this important document.

In the absence of this official county register information has been obtained from a variety of sources. The most important reference document has been the unpublished list of Isle of Wight registrations in the original DL-series 1903 – 1935 (2nd edition 2008) produced by Don Vincent and Chris Roberts. This document, which concentrates on buses, charabancs and coaches but also includes some information on other motor vehicles, was produced following extensive research by the PSV Circle. Other detailed material has been obtained from contemporary magazine and local newspaper reports, a personal scrapbook which was compiled by Ryde resident Miss Benest and various Isle of Wight local history books. The photographs have been assembled from the collections of many organisations and individuals, including the Isle of Wight Record Office, the Carisbrooke Castle Museum and the Isle of Wight Council Museum plus the author's collection (see list of photographers).

Clear images of Isle of Wight cars, motorcycles and commercial vehicles prior to the First World War, especially those showing DL number plates, are quite rare. Pictures of early buses and charabancs are slightly more common, however. This is mainly because these vehicles had great novelty value in the Edwardian decade and formed the subject of several popular postcards. Some of these postcards (e.g. of Isle of Wight Express Motor Syndicate Ltd. motor buses at Ryde Esplanade and other locations) had wide appeal to holidaymakers and were sold in large numbers over several years. Others, showing close up views of buses and charabancs with their passengers, were produced in smaller numbers by enterprising local photographers for the people who had just experienced a journey in a "horse-less carriage", in many cases for the first time in their lives.

A number of pioneer local car owners formed the Isle of Wight Motorists' Association in November 1903, with headquarters at Warburton's Hotel, Quay Street, Newport (now Calvert's Hotel). In 1905/06 the committee members were:-

Thomas B H Cochrane, Deputy Governor of the Isle of Wight (President) (DL 68)
Major C P Dean, The Towers, Yarmouth (Vice President) (DL 25)
Dr R H Armstrong, Five Rocks, Blackgang (DL 17 and DL 19)
E C Carnt, Park Gate, East Cowes
Captain W Corke, Castle Mount, West Cowes
Colonel W H Gordon, Barsham Lodge, Sandown (DL 3)
Dr Lowe, The Rays, Newport
Major Somerset Leeke, Sea View, Yarmouth
Sir John Thornycroft, Steyn, Bembridge
J Lee White (son of John Samuel White), Seafield, Ryde

Some early Isle of Wight DL registrations recorded in copies of Motor Car Journal/The Motor Car and Motor Cycle Directory of Great Britain and Ireland in 1906 were:-

DL 2 – Mrs G H Harrison, Thornton, near Ryde
DL 3 – Col. W H Gordon, Barsham Lodge, Sandown
DL 4 – P Craven Hall, Beldornie Tower, Ryde
DL 12 – Douglas Atkey, High Street, Cowes
DL 17 – Dr. Robert H Armstrong, Five Rocks, Blackgang
DL 19 – Dr. Robert H Armstrong, Five Rocks, Blackgang (motorcycle)
DL 25 – Major Dean, The Towers, Yarmouth
DL 31 – A C Clark, Ryde
DL 32 – A C Clark, Ryde

During the Edwardian decade and up to the outbreak of the First World War motor vehicles on the Isle of Wight were few and far between and were greatly outnumbered by horse-drawn vehicles. Initially they were viewed with suspicion and even hostility by many Islanders. There were some cases of horses being frightened by noisy motor cars and motorcycles and several people wrote letters to the local newspapers complaining about the various perceived dangers they presented to pedestrians and passengers in horse-drawn vehicles.

Local opinion was not totally opposed to the new motor vehicles, however, and car owners and their supporters worked hard to explain the many benefits that they would bring to Island families and businesses. King Edward VII, a keen pioneer motorist who owned several Daimler cars, was a great advocate of motoring and his support was a major factor in promoting the development and increased popularity of this form of transport across the whole country. An example of His Majesty's active involvement in this field was to offer his royal patronage to the Automobile Club of Great Britain and Ireland, which became the Royal Automobile Club (RAC) on 8th March 1907.

In April 1905, following a bold and rapid initiative led by Charles Campbell Macklin, who canvassed Lord Onslow and Alderman A. Millward, the Mayor of Ryde for their support, Isle of Wight Express Motor Syndicate Ltd. (IWEMS) launched a network of local bus services with four new Milnes-Daimler open top double deck motor buses, registered DL 75 to 78. Within three months the firm had acquired a fleet of nine such vehicles, with the addition of DL 79 to 81, DL 109 and DL 110. Each bus was able to accommodate 36 seated passengers. This was truly a pioneer bus operator. With its main depot in Ryde the firm provided a number of services to Newport, Shanklin, Seaview, Bembridge and East Cowes. Carisbrooke Castle and Osborne House were very popular destinations and the firm introduced various innovative features such as discounted books of tickets and the carriage of letters and parcels.

The first season of operation up to October 1905 was quite successful with the buses covering 89,000 miles and carrying around 175,000 passengers. However, the 24hp buses were found to be somewhat underpowered for the Island's hilly roads and the whole fleet was sold to a London operator. Over the winter of 1905/06 the services were suspended and IWEMS purchased nine replacement vehicles. Seven 30-seat Milnes-Daimler 28/30hp charabancs and two FIAT 36-seat double deck buses were purchased and brought into service in the Spring of 1906. The

Milnes-Daimler charabancs, with bodies built by George Mulliss and Co. of Ryde, were registered as DL 129, DL 130 and DL 133 to DL 137. The FIAT double deck buses were registered as DL 131 and DL 132. In addition to the Milnes-Daimlers and FIATs there were two Wolseley-Siddeley 30hp double deck buses with Dodson bodywork which were delivered in the summer of 1906 and registered in Portsmouth. These vehicles formed the main part of the IWEMS fleet until the firm ceased trading towards the end of 1907. For a few months in 1907 the firm also operated four leased second-hand 30-seat Thornycroft 24hp charabancs (DL 203 to DL 206).

One of Isle of Wight Express Motor Syndicate Ltd.'s initial fleet of nine Milnes-Daimler double deck buses is pictured above. DL 78 was one of the four vehicles involved in the launch of the IWEMS bus services in Ryde in April 1905. It is shown here in a 1905 postcard photo taken in Victoria Avenue, Shanklin with a full load of holiday makers from Sandown and Shanklin bound for Newport and Carisbrooke Castle.

The photograph above shows the interior of Bailey's Garage in Shanklin, c.1904. It can be seen that car servicing and repair work was very labour intensive at that time. The dismantled vehicle at the front of the picture is thought to be a Mors car (AN 258) built in Belgium which belonged to the Bailey family. Young Harry Bailey is on the extreme right.

According to a report in the Isle of Wight County Press on 29th July 1905 the inaugural motoring meeting of the Isle of Wight Motorists' Association was held at Carisbrooke Castle on 27th July 1905 with a "Motor Gymkhana".

Motor car gymkhana at Carisbrooke Castle

The bowling green of Carisbrooke Castle was the scene on Thursday afternoon of what for the Island was a novelty, namely, a motor car gymkhana, held under the auspices of the Isle of Wight Motorists' Association. That this Association was able to make so auspicious a commencement with competitions, interesting to motorists and non-motorists alike, and to demonstrate the reality of its existence, was in large measure due to the President (Mr T.B.H. Cochrane, M.V.O.), Deputy Governor of the Island, and Lady Adela Cochrane, by whose kind invitation the gymkhana was held at so popular a centre and under such favourable auspices. Island motorists were present in considerable numbers, and many others responded to the invitation of the Deputy Governor and Lady Adela, a fashionable company witnessing the various events. Princess Elizabeth of Roumania, attended by Miss Bulteel and Miss Collett, was amongst those present. Among the members of the Association and other motorists present, in addition to the Deputy Governor and Lady Adela Cochrane, were Major C.P. Dean (Vice President), Mrs. Bird (Slatwoods), Mrs. G.H. Harrison (Thornton), Sir John I. Thornycroft, Dr. Armstrong, Dr. Lowe, Dr. G. Adkins, Col. W.H.G. Gordon, Col. Hamilton, J.P., Major and Mrs. Gordon Brodie, Capt. E. du Boulay, Capt. and Mrs. Chamberlain, Capt. and Mrs. Alexander-Sinclair, Mr. and Mrs. Mackenzie, Capt. Hamilton, Messrs. E.C. Carnt (East Cowes), J. Lee White, W.P. Brigstocke (Ryde), S. Charlton (St. Catherines). F.J. Dean (Beaulieu), J.T. Dickinson (Yarmouth), Mr. and Mrs. H. Garle, Mr. P. Craven Hall, Mr. S.M. Mellor (St. Helens), Mr. E. Ward and others.

Some of the finest cars on the road were present and there was a very good entry in the interesting competitions, which evidenced very skilful driving on the part of owners and others taking part, and graceful manoeuvring on the part of the cars. The finals in the competitions resulted as follows:-

Bending race: drive forward 100 yards, between posts 7 feet apart and return; breaking a post disqualified – Major C.P. Dean beat Mr E.C. Carnt.

Passenger race: cars start on 160 yards course, to pick up three passengers at intervals and return to winning post, driver opening and closing the car door for passengers – Major C. Gordon Brodie beat Mr. E.C. Carnt.

Coach-house race: cars start on 160 yards course to coach-house, driver opens coach-house, runs his car in house and out again, and returns to winning post – Mr. W.P. Brigstocke's chauffeur beat Mr. T.B.H. Cochrane.

Bending race: driving backwards over 100 yards course, breaking a post disqualified – Sir John I. Thornycroft beat Mrs. Bird's chauffeur.

The judge was Col. W. H. G. Gordon; starter A. H. P. Clarke; and stewards Mr Cochrane and Major Dean. At the close the prizes, given by the Association, were distributed by Lady Adela Cochrane. Major Dean proposed a hearty vote of thanks to the Deputy Governor and Lady Adela Cochrane for their extreme kindness in connection with the arranging of their first motoring gymkhana and he hoped it would be the precursor of many such pleasant meetings and of the prosperity of the Isle of Wight Motorists' Association. They had all enjoyed themselves very much there, and the proceedings had been a great success (applause). The company were entertained at tea on the bowling green during the proceedings by the Deputy Governor and Lady Adela.

Early motorists and motorcyclists tended to be male owners of successful local businesses, doctors or retired army officers. One exception was Miss Cleone de Heveningham Benest, a young woman of independent means who lived with her mother and grandmother in Ryde. Miss Benest kept a detailed personal scrapbook from 1905 to 1911 and this provides some fascinating evidence of the cars she owned, drove and maintained in her own workshop. The scrapbook also reveals Miss Benest's great interest in motoring generally and contains correspondence with some of the key figures of motor manufacturing and bus operation, including F.W. Lanchester, S.F. Edge (Napier), Colonel Crompton and Douglas Mackenzie.

At a time before women were granted the vote Miss Benest was one of the first ladies to pass the motor engineering examination held by the City and Guilds of London in 1908, when she was the only female candidate. She attended many meetings of the Institution of Automobile Engineers, even though women were not permitted to become members at that time. On the Island Miss Benest was an active motorist and a keen promoter of the benefits of motoring. She tried to arrange a meeting of the Hamphire Automobile Club on the Island. Interestingly, a letter in the scrapbook shows that her invitation was declined, very politely, on the grounds that "it would have been too difficult for their members to transport their vehicles across the Solent".

The above photograph shows an Edwardian joint railways tow barge unloading vehicles from the Island at the former Wightlink slipway at Portsmouth. A Mercedes car is about to be driven down the exit planks.

Miss Benest took every opportunity to drive a wide range of cars and commercial vehicles and was allowed to drive several Milnes-Daimler and Thornycroft buses belonging to the Isle of Wight Express Motor Syndicate Ltd. under the tutelage of Fred Crinage between 1905 and 1907. In 1910 Miss Benest was charged with driving in central Ryde in an unsafe manner. However the case was dismissed by local magistrates after consideration of all the evidence.

The Isle of Wight County Press carried some interesting advertisements relating to early motoring on the Island. The 9/1/1904 issue contained the following advertisement:

> *Motor-cars, motor-cycles, for sale or hire. The only works in the Island devoted to automobiles; driving taught; several good second hand vehicles; early delivery of all leading machines – Telephone: 166Y CLARK, Motor Works, George Street, Ryde*

The following advert appeared on the front page of several issues around the end of 1903/ beginning of 1904:

> *"THE HUMBERETTE"*
> *5 HP LIGHT MOTOR CAR*
> *125 GUINEAS*
>
> *Sole agent for the Isle of Wight*
> *D. MARVIN, Motor Depot, 9 Union Street, Ryde where car can now be seen and trial given to intending buyers.*
>
> *Prompt delivery of these popular cars from stock orders*
>
> *D. MARVIN, RYDE, SOLE AGENT FOR HUMBER MOTORS*

Second hand motor vehicles were also offered for sale through the local newspaper, for example this advert which appeared in the 23/4/1904 issue:

> *FOR SALE – CYCLES AND MOTORS*
>
> *Humber Special Motor Bicycle, 2.75hp*
>
> *Free engine clutch, spring pillar, spares, lamp, number plates, luggage carrier, etc. Splendid condition*
>
> *Write T.R. – County Press, Newport*

MARTIN BROS.

Carriage & Motor Works,

ALBERT STREET, VENTNOR,

Telephone: No. 72 Y.

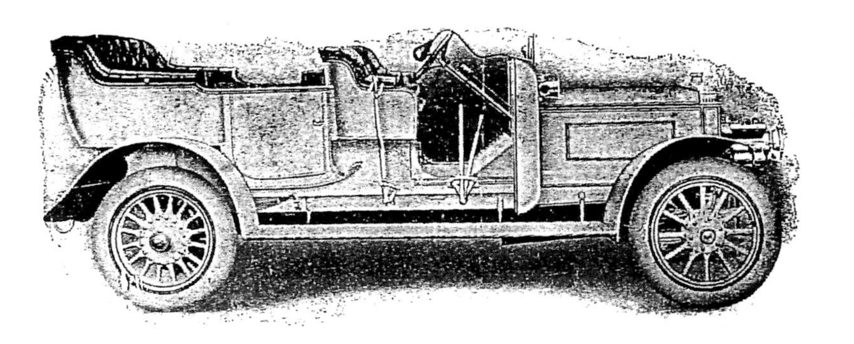

EVERY CLASS OF REPAIRS.

Stockists of "Prowodnik" Tyres. Garage and all Requisites.

CARS FOR HIRE

Another very early Isle of Wight garage was Martin Brothers of Ventnor. This period advertisement is believed to date from around 1912.

DL 1 or DL 7? *The earliest known Isle of Wight-registered motor vehicle to be photographed was a 2-seat Darracq 15hp car. The Darracq chassis, which was built around 1901/1902, was originally fitted with a Lacre side entrance body. This was subsequently replaced by the stylish body in the photo which was manufactured locally by R. Bird Cheverton of Newport. The original body was transferred to the same owner's 40hp Austin. The photograph was taken in 1908.*

Not all DL-registered motor vehicles were owned and used on the Isle of Wight during this period. The largest known example of this practice relates to DL registrations made by Douglas Mackenzie. Mackenzie was an early public transport consultant based in Westminster who was employed by Isle of Wight Express Motor Syndicate Ltd. in 1907 in a desperate attempt to reverse the fortunes of this ailing bus operator. Shortly after he started working for IWEMS Mackenzie leased eight second hand Thornycroft charabancs from London Motor Omnibus Co. Ltd. and re-registered these vehicles as DL 203 to DL 210 (inclusive). DL 203 to DL 206 with conventional 30-seat charabanc bodies joined the IWEMS fleet and the other four vehicles were allocated to bus companies on the mainland that Mackenzie was connected with.

Isle of Wight Express Motor Syndicate Ltd. ceased operating local bus services on the Island by the end of 1907 but Mackenzie continued to reserve and confirm further DL registration numbers until 1913. He matched these registrations to buses, charabancs and taxis working in Worthing, Torquay and Clacton. Numbers which are known to have been obtained by Mackenzie in this way are DL 254 to DL 256, DL 261, DL 371, DL 381 to DL 384, DL 401 to DL 403, DL 493, DL 621 and DL 701 to DL 706. In addition Mackenzie is known to have reserved DL 262, DL 263, DL 301 and DL 302 (possibly intended for IWEMS if it had survived into 1908) but these were not issued to him. Mackenzie went on to have a glittering career in bus operation. He is best known as one of the founders and driving forces behind the successful development of Southdown Motor Services Ltd. in Sussex and Hampshire in the 1920s.

During the First World War (1914 to 1918) the vast majority of road vehicles being manufactured were produced for the War Department. Up to 1915 it was still possible for a limited number of cars, motorcycles and vans to be purchased by firms and individuals for civilian use. Lloyd George's bill of March 1915 suggested that all engineering work should be confined to war work, thus causing most motor manufacture for the private market to cease. This took immediate effect and was noted in the board meeting notes of the ABC company, for example. ABC continued to develop their 500cc motorcycle in the hope of War Department contracts, but few were made after March 1915. Around 90% of despatch rider motorcycles were manufactured by Triumph and Douglas. Cars such as Sunbeam (built by the Rover company) and Crossley were used as staff cars, ambulances, etc.

There are very limited records of new vehicles with DL registrations around this time. It seems likely that numbers had probably reached around DL 1500 by the start of 1916 and that very few further local vehicle registrations took place in Newport until the war ended in November 1918. Isle of Wight businesses and individuals had to manage with rail transport, existing steam-powered and motor vehicles, bicycles and horse drawn transport until domestic market restrictions were removed.

DL 12 *This is a Humber 3hp single speed motorcycle with passenger trailer c.1904. It was an 'all chain drive' machine at a time when most motorcycles were belt-driven. Passenger trailers were normally built by separate specialist manufacturers.*

DL 20 *Dennis four-cylinder basic tourer pictured outside the Royal Marine Hotel, Belgrave Road, Ventnor c.1904. This car had a windscreen and hood but little side protection in bad weather. Dennis Brothers of Guildford produced many sturdy and reliable cars and commercial vehicles from 1899 to 1915. From 1915 onwards the company ceased making cars and concentrated entirely on manufacturing lorries, fire engines, buses, charabancs and other commercial vehicles.*

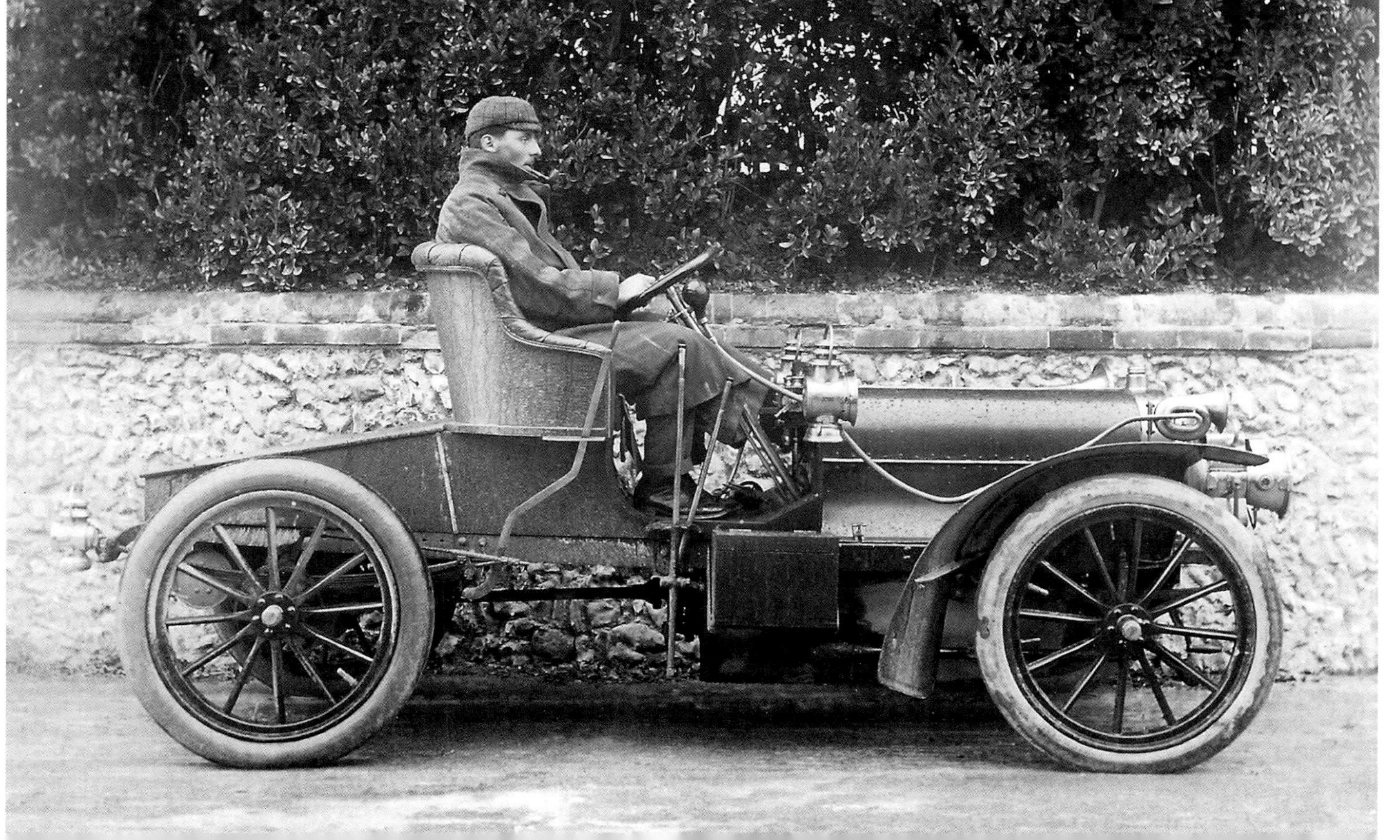

***DL 27** Argyll 2-seat car, probably a 16hp four cylinder of c.1904/1905. At this time there were two, three and four cylinder Argylls, and each type had a completely different radiator shape. Front and side views of this very early Isle of Wight-registered car. Unusually the vehicle was fitted with twin horns which were operated manually - one by the driver and the other by the passenger!*

DL 45 *Peugeot wagonette. This vehicle, previously thought to be a Daimler, has now been identified conclusively as a Type 29 2-cylinder 12hp Peugeot. It was almost certainly manufactured in 1901 or 1902 and given an Isle of Wight registration number in early 1904. From the sign on the side of the wagonette it can be seen that the vehicle was used to operate a regular service from Newport to Carisbrooke. The photo was taken outside the former convent in Carisbrooke High Street near the bottom of Cedar Hill.*

DL 66 *International Charette. This small 2-seat car was built around 1902. These smart vehicles were manufactured for the International Motor Car Company Ltd. by Allard and Company Ltd. of Coventry until 1902 when Allard combined with the Birmingham Motor Manufacturing and Supply Company. Walter William Sirkett and his wife Mabel Louise Glover Swan Sirkett and one of their three sons are seen posing proudly with their vehicle at the Seaview Hotel which was owned by Mr Sirkett. The picture was probably taken in 1905.*

DL 6x? *In addition, Walter Sirkett owned this MMC 7hp single-cylinder car at around that time. Unfortunately it is not possible to see the whole number plate. It could be DL 6 or more likely DL sixty something. The vehicle was manufactured in 1902 or 1903. It was also photographed at the Seaview Hotel with Sirkett and a friend or relative. There is an unusual reflection of the photographer and several onlookers in the windscreen of the other car. Note the distinctive tubular chassis and chain drive.*

DL 68 *Dennis car. The photograph shows the vehicle with its owner Thomas B.H. Cochrane who was Deputy Governor of the Isle of Wight in the Edwardian period. Mr. Cochrane and his wife Lady Adela were both strong advocates for motor transport. Mr Cochrane was President of the Isle of Wight Motorists' Association. Lady Adela Cochrane famously launched the Isle of Wight Express Motor Syndicate Ltd.'s pioneering network of local bus services in Ryde on 13th April 1905. This photo was possibly taken during that same year.*

DL 85 *Humber 10/12hp car. This fine motor car was a 'Coventry' Humber which was probably manufactured in 1905. Humber also had a factory at Beeston at that time and the company's 'de luxe' models were generally built there and were referred to as 'Beeston Humbers'. The people in the photo are unknown but the charming message on the rear of the original postcard, postmarked 'Newport August 1906' read "Uncle Gus had a 36 mile drive in this car".*

DL 79 *Isle of Wight Express Motor Syndicate double deck Milnes-Daimler bus is seen climbing Brading High Street. It was on its way from Ryde to Shanklin with a full load of passengers on a hot sunny day in 1905.*

DL-85

DL 130 *Milnes-Daimler 28/30hp charabanc. This vehicle, with locally built bodywork by George Mullis and Co. of Nelson Street, Ryde was delivered new to Isle of Wight Express Motor Syndicate Ltd. in March 1906. It was sold in February 1908 after the firm had gone into liquidation.*

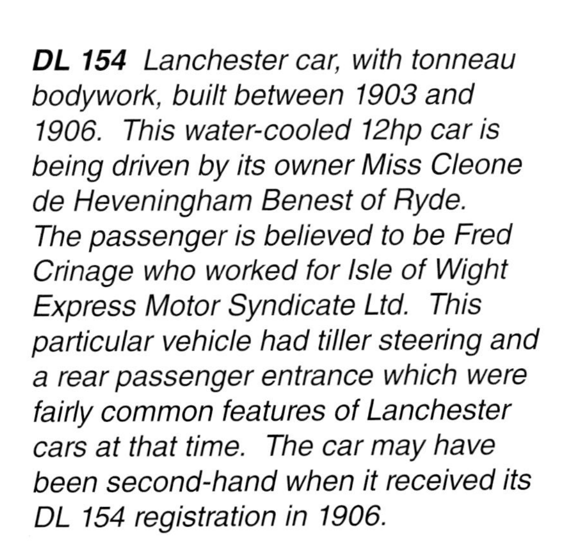

DL 154 *Lanchester car, with tonneau bodywork, built between 1903 and 1906. This water-cooled 12hp car is being driven by its owner Miss Cleone de Heveningham Benest of Ryde. The passenger is believed to be Fred Crinage who worked for Isle of Wight Express Motor Syndicate Ltd. This particular vehicle had tiller steering and a rear passenger entrance which were fairly common features of Lanchester cars at that time. The car may have been second-hand when it received its DL 154 registration in 1906.*

DL 203 *Thornycroft charabanc. In May 1907 this vehicle was leased by Douglas Mackenzie and re-registered as DL 203 for Isle of Wight Express Motor Syndicate Ltd. It saw active service on the Isle of Wight until the end of the year when it was transferred to Sussex Motor Road Car Co. Ltd. in Worthing, where this photograph was taken. Note the steeply tiered seating arrangement. The vehicle had a more conventional charabanc body when it was operated by IWEMS on the Isle of Wight.*

DL 205 *This is believed to be a De Dion Bouton car, c.1903. According to the handwritten note on the rear of the original postcard the photograph was taken at the 1926 Newport carnival with Pritchard Flanders driving the car. Registration number DL 205 was initially issued to an IWEMS Thornycroft charabanc in 1907 and is a good example of how some early DL numbers were re-issued by the Isle of Wight County Council when vehicles left the Island or were scrapped.*

DL 299 *Gardner Serpollet steam-powered covered charabanc. In December 1908 Arthur Creeth of Nettlestone purchased and registered this vehicle which he fitted with a 14-seat body built in his own blacksmith's workshop. The charabanc entered service on Creeth's bus route from Ryde to Seaview in March 1909.*

DL 341 *Vauxhall car being used for driving lesson. According to the text on the rear of the original postcard this picture shows Mr R. Gallop instructing a pupil in the yard at the Eight Bells Public House, Carisbrooke. The original chassis is believed to date from around 1907 with the body appearing to be a more recent addition.*

DL 367 *Minerva charabanc. This vehicle was built in Antwerp, Belgium in 1908 with a powerful sleeve-valve engine of at least 4000cc to American design and bodied as a luxury chauffeur-driven private car. The vehicle was purchased by E.H. Crinage, of Ventnor, probably late 1913 or early 1914: the original body was removed; the chassis was extended rearwards; and a locally constructed charabanc body was built, seating a maximum of eleven people plus driver. It is claimed to have been the first charabanc to operate from Ventnor. The photograph was taken outside the Royal Marine Hotel, Belgrave Road in Ventnor. A folding hood (stacked behind the passengers) was available for inclement weather.*

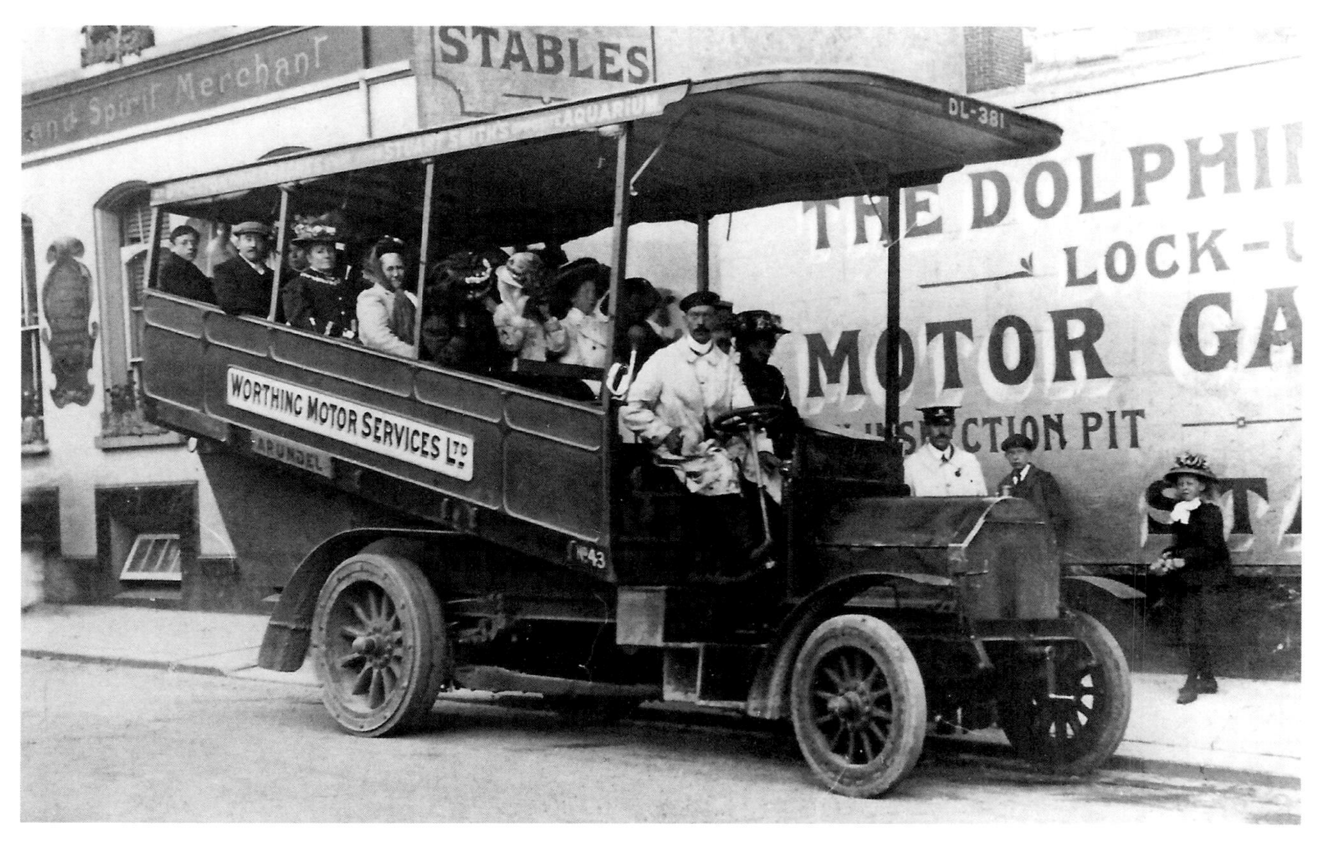

DL 381 *Milnes-Daimler 20hp charabanc. This 30-seat vehicle was purchased by Douglas Mackenzie from London Westminster Omnibus Company, the owners of Hastings and St. Leonards Motor Omnibus Company and re-registered DL 381 in August 1908. It is not believed to have seen active service on the Isle of Wight and was operated by Worthing Motor Services Ltd. in Sussex for several years from 1909 to 1915.*

DL 387 *Ariel 500cc motorcycle combination, c.1909. This was a belt-driven machine and almost certainly single speed, with no gears. The magneto fitted is an 'open' Bosch (i.e. with open ends). Advance and retard of the spark was by a tank operated lever visible in the photograph. The wicker sidecar was typical for that period. Wicker was chosen for its lightness as against a coachbuilt version.*

DL 415 *New Pick car, c.1909/1910, probably around 14hp. Many motor manufacturers at that time tended to sell their cars within a fairly local area. The New Pick was built in Stamford, Lincolnshire and went against this trend. The firm's vehicles managed to find favour in small numbers across quite a wide geographical area.*

DL-415

DL 432 *The only known royal vehicle with a 'DL' registration number is shown in this photograph, which was taken at Kensington Palace, c.1912. DL 432 was a high quality four-cylinder or six-cylinder Vauxhall landaulette which was built around 1910. Standing next to the car is William Ayers who was a royal chauffeur for many years before the Second World War. It is thought that this vehicle was mainly used for transporting Princess Beatrice and members of her family between London and the Isle of Wight when she was Governor of the Isle of Wight. Princess Beatrice, the youngest daughter of Queen Victoria, often spent periods of around three months living at Carisbrooke Castle and working on the Isle of Wight. Driving Princess Beatrice to and from the Isle of Wight was a major part of William Ayers' duties. He retired to the Island in 1946. The other two royal vehicles are a 1911 Vauxhall Prince Henry tourer (V 1237) and a Daimler cabriolet, c.1911, about 25hp.*

DL 542 or DL 543 *This is a Scout car, possibly a 20hp model, manufactured in Salisbury around 1908. The photo was taken in Ventnor with members of the local Aviation Committee. They are known to have organised at least one programme of air races in 1911 in the very early days of flying.*

DL 552 *De Dion Bouton landaulette car, c.1912. This luxurious vehicle was owned by an unknown wealthy Niton resident. His or her uniformed chauffeur is seen opening a rear passenger door.*

DL 668 *Morgan 3-wheeler. This well-laden little vehicle is a Morgan standard model 8 from around 1913. The Morgan 8 was produced from 1910 to 1916 with a V-2 961cc engine, probably by JAP. Note that it has no front door or passenger enclosure. Several body styles were available, some giving rather more safety and weather protection!*

DL 723 *'FN' (Fabrique Nationale) 800cc motorcycle. This powerful motorcycle was manufactured in Belgium from around 1907 to 1910 and registered on the Isle of Wight by Edwin (Ted) Creeth around 1911. The engine had a very distinctive appearance with the four cylinders "in line".*

DL 730 *Germain 4-seat tourer. This is believed to be a Germain car, manufactured in Belgium around 1906. Many slightly later Germain cars had an oval radiator but some of the earlier models had radiators like the one in this photograph.*

DL 970 *Triumph 500cc side valve motorcycle. Manufactured in Coventry this motorcycle had a single speed with no gears. It was fitted with a hub clutch on the rear wheel. The model dates from around 1911 and was a popular motorcycle in Britain at that time.*

Ford Model T landaulette taxi in Sandown.
This taxi, built around 1910/1911, was owned by H.P. Colenutt. It is shown outside Colenutt's Garage in the Boadway, Sandown. H.P. Colenutt went on to operate a charabanc business (Star) from 1919 to 1931. This firm was taken over by Moss Motor Tours in 1931 when Colenutt became a director of that company.

DL 1056 *Ford Model T landaulette taxi. This vehicle was built in 1912 or 1913 and registered on the Isle of Wight at that time. In this photo it is being driven by Herbie Wheeler who operated a local taxi business in the Porchfield area in the 1920s. The rear soft top roof could be put down in fine weather if requested.*

DL 1338? *The Ford Model T van shown above was probably built in 1914 just before the First World War. It was owned by Wray and Sons, Bakers and Confectioners, of Newport. In the photograph it is being driven by Herbert Foss (father of author Keir Foss) who left school in 1916 at the age of 14 and started a three year apprenticeship with Wray and Sons. Herbert Foss was aged just 15 when he was pictured driving the firm's left hand drive delivery van in 1917!*

DL 1353 *Ford Model T van. This Ford delivery van is also believed to have been built in 1914. It was owned by Booth and Son, Bakers and Confectioners, of Ventnor. This picture was probably taken during the First World War when women were employed to carry out many jobs normally carried out by men in peace time.*

DL 190? *The impressive Rolls Royce landaulette in the above photograph is believed to date from around 1910. It was being driven by Mr Wilf Barton who owned Barton's Taxis of Newport. Mr Barton had a special agreement to be the only taxi operator permitted to serve Newport railway station. Although it has not been proved conclusively, it is thought that this vehicle was probably registered as DL 190, and was originally owned by the Oglander family of Nunwell Manor, near Brading. The vehicle may have been carrying a replacement body when this picture was taken around 1930.*

DL 753 *One of the first vehicles to be owned by Coombes Brothers of Shanklin was this attractive De Dietrich 11-seat charabanc. Coombes Brothers was a successful coach operator up to the late 1940s. Unusually the firm also operated pleasure flights in the 1930s from a small airfield in Shanklin. The vehicle was probably first registered in 1913 and the photograph is believed to have been taken in 1914. It was taken outside Shanklin post office which is displaying a poster inviting local residents to invest in war loans.*

3 DL VEHICLES 1919 to 1929

After the First World War ended on 11th November 1918 Britain underwent massive economic, social and political changes. For the previous four years a huge proportion of the country's research, development and manufacturing resources had been devoted to supporting military activities. Suddenly, following a period of serious austerity, there was a major opportunity for firms to switch production from weapons and military vehicles to products for the civilian population. In addition there were many army vehicles which had become surplus to requirements and these were returned to their previous owners or sold to entrepreneurs who were keen to rebuild their businesses. The general atmosphere was that it was time to build a country fit for heroes and there was a widespread appetite within the population for mechanical innovation and economic growth.

Large numbers of army lorries, buses, cars and motorcycles were overhauled and brought into service for a wide range of civilian activities. Some of these vehicles were purchased by former soldiers who had acquired driving and vehicle maintenance skills during the war and were keen to set up their own taxi, bus operating and haulage firms. Several major vehicle overhaul and disposal depots were established where they were either stripped and reconditioned for sale at auction, or broken up for spares. In South East England Kempton Park racecourse near Sunbury and several London squares were used as temporary 'dumps' where redundant vehicles were parked for many months awaiting sale or scrapping. The huge War Department depot at Cippenham, near Slough, received many thousands of such vehicles which were driven or more often towed from the continent and brought by sea via Kent. The Cippenham depot 'recycled' many thousands of vehicles including large numbers of former despatch rider motorcycles which were mainly Triumph and Douglas machines.

In addition new vehicles began to roll off the factory production lines again and these were eagerly bought by businesses and families who had often had to manage with horse-drawn vehicles or bicycles during the difficult war years. Political, economic and social conditions were right for a major modernisation of British society. Boosted by the increasing availability of cheaper and more reliable mass-produced vehicles from major manufacturers such as Ford, Morris and Rover, motor vehicles started to become more numerous as horse-drawn transport continued to decline. When supplies of new British vehicles could not keep pace with demand, imported vehicles (often from America) were made available. Sometimes a chassis would be bought from abroad and then fitted with a lorry or charabanc body by a local coachbuilder.

On the Isle of Wight around 1,000 newly-registered DL vehicles appeared on local roads between January 1919 and December 1921, bringing numbers up to DL 2500. There was a great deal of variety in the types of vehicles acquired. There were many lorries, vans, cars, motorcycles, buses, charabancs, taxis, brakes, traction engines, emergency vehicles and tipper trucks being bought. Vehicles were supplied by a number of Island garages who operated dealerships for the main motor manufacturers. Frank Cheverton Ltd. of Newport was the main dealer for Ford cars and commercial vehicles. Some other major garages during the 1920s were Fountain Garage (Cowes), Smith and Whitehead (Newport), Fowlers (Newport), Seafield Garage (Seaview) and G.K. Nash (Ventnor). A major supplier of motorcycles was C.F. Stagg of South Street, Newport.

One very significant local development immediately after the First World War was the establishment of a factory at Somerton producing an early type of motor scooter – the ABC Skootamota. Designed by the prolific inventor Granville Bradshaw the Skootamota had a strong tubular steel frame and two small wheels. It was powered by a simple one cylinder ABC 125cc engine positioned above the rear wheel. This engine had been used successfully as an auxiliary engine in various aircraft during the war. Following the termination of some military contracts the important shipbuilder J.S. White Ltd. found that it had surplus factory accommodation at Somerton, Cowes (adjacent to the former aerodrome). The firm of Gilbert Campling Ltd. saw the opportunity of manufacturing and marketing this small motorcycle and obtained agreements from ABC and J.S. White Ltd. to assemble the vehicles on the Island.

Period advertisements show that this vehicle, which could

achieve speeds of around 15mph, was promoted to men and women. The design of the low platform and ease of use meant that it was quite practical for women to drive when wearing long skirts, which were fashionable at that time. Around 3,500 ABC Skootamotas were produced and sold between 1919 and 1922 and it was considered to be the most successful of a number of similar vehicles which were manufactured by several British firms. The picture on the right shows an advertisement for the ABC Skootamota. This appeared in the magazine *Punch* in September 1919.

is made by

GILBERT CAMPLING, LTD.

(Members M.T.A.)

1 Albemarle Street, Piccadilly, London, W.1

Write for Booklet E.

The Roads Act 1920 came into effect on 1st January 1921. This important piece of legislation introduced individual vehicle licences which had to be renewed annually. These road fund licences were required to be displayed. There were also provisions for licensing taxis and buses whereby operators were issued with an approved number of licences for a maximum number of vehicles that could be used at the same time. In addition the Act made it compulsory for traction engines and tractors to be issued with registration numbers by county councils. The Isle of Wight County Council was required to reissue existing 'DL' registration numbers, to issue new numbers for all new DL-registered motor vehicles from January 1921 onwards and to keep an official register of all numbers issued. Motor vehicle owners became liable for heavy fines if they were found to be driving their vehicle without displaying their correct tax disc or number plates clearly.

The 1920s witnessed a major growth in the provision of local bus services and charabanc excursions. There was very limited regulation in this period and many new firms were set up to meet the travel needs of residents and visitors. Several firms operated in direct competition with each other on the busier routes (e.g. Cowes to Newport, Newport to Ryde and Newport to Carisbrooke) and there were many incidents of vehicles racing to pick up waiting passengers and attempting to delay the vehicles of competitors. The three largest operators were Vectis Bus Company (which became Southern Vectis in 1929), Wavell's Enterprise Bus Service (which continued to operate a frequent daily service from Newport to Sandown until 1951) and Brown's Bus Service (which operated several routes from Newport to the West Wight from 1925 to 1935). Round-the-Island charabanc tours and shorter excursions became very popular with holidaymakers in the summer months and provided a very good source of income for many firms including H.P. Colenutt (Star) of Sandown, Coombes Brothers of Shanklin, G.K. Nash of Ventnor, H. Paul and Son of Ryde and Saunders (Yellow Cars) of Yarmouth.

By the end of 1929 Isle of Wight registered motor vehicles had reached DL 6750. This was a Singer 'Junior' half-ton van which was owned by Mr H.J. Dore of Sandown. Taking into account the

DL 1461? *This large Leyland charabanc is believed to be DL 1461, which was owned by Fountain Garage Ltd., of Cowes until January 1921. This vehicle, named "Island Queen", was almost certainly an ex-War Department vehicle which was used for transporting British troops during the First World War. It was registered in June 1919 and was converted from 36 seats to 32 seats in September 1919. The photograph was taken outside Gurnard post office close to the start of an excursion from Cowes to Alum Bay and the Needles.*

number of vehicles which had been scrapped or transferred to the mainland and the reallocation of some of the earlier numbers to new vehicles it is estimated that there were probably in the region of 4,000 DL-registered vehicles in use on the Island at this time. Cars, motorcycles, commercial vehicles, buses and charabancs were all becoming more numerous but they were probably still outnumbered by horse-drawn vehicles which remained popular with many firms and families especially for shorter journeys. Car ownership remained comparatively rare. Motorcycles (often fitted with passenger sidecars) provided a more affordable form of transport for many people and probably outnumbered cars on the Island at the start of the 1930s.

DL 1463 *Sharpe's picnic party was photographed in Ventnor on 9th July 1919. The 26-seat solid-tyred Dennis 'A-type' charabanc was owned by A.H. Creeth (Premier Motors) of Nettlestone. The chassis was built by Dennis Brothers in Guildford possibly during the war as a 3-ton 'Subsidy' lorry. It is not known who built the replacement charabanc body shown in the photograph. This may have been produced by Arthur Creeth in Nettlestone who is known to have built several other charabanc bodies for his vehicles.*

DL 1560 *This is an early ABC Skootamota, produced at Somerton in the first few months of 1919. The photograph shows the machine with its owner, Mr H.H. Burrows, who lived in Southend, Essex. The Skootamota had just won a scooter class race in the Westcliff-on-Sea Speed Trials in July 1919. ABC may have registered a number of Skootamotas with DL registrations when they came out of the Isle of Wight factory, ready for delivery to mainland dealers and immediate use by customers. This was a fairly common practice for motor vehicle manufacturers in Britain up to the 1920s.*

DL 1474 *Reg Weeks (who lived with his family at Calbourne Mill) and his friend Bill Ablitt riding pillion on their Triumph Model H 550cc motorcycle on an outing to Ventnor, c.1920. Around 18,000 Model H's were manufactured for the British army during the First World War for use by despatch riders. Years later, the children of Calbourne were permitted to push this machine up the long incline at Calbourne Mill and "ride" it back down the slope.*

DL 1570 *Edward H. Crinage of Ventnor was a very enterprising and successful businessman. In addition to his garage and charabanc business in Ventnor Crinage established a successful road haulage operation in the Midlands. Shortly after the end of the war Crinage secured a very large contract to deliver new motor car engines from the Hotchkiss factory in Coventry to the Morris factory in Cowley, Oxford. This contract existed for many years. In this photograph Crinage's Daimler Type W three-and-a-half-ton lorry registered DL 1570 is seen with a trailer collecting a load of new engines prior to transporting them to Oxford.*

DL 1690 *Left hand drive Ford Model T four-seat tourer. This car was probably built between 1918 and 1920 and has been modified with the addition of a number of accessories, including the oil side lights and mounting brackets which are not genuine Ford. The large domed nuts holding the wheels to the hubs were a Michelin conversion to enable wheels to be changed rather than mend a puncture in place.*

DL 1696 *Henderson four-cylinder 10hp motorcycle combination. This powerful American machine would have been very rare on the Isle of Wight in the early 1920s. Note the distinctive curved front forks and electric lights.*

DL 21xx? *Unfortunately relatively little is known of this very attractive Armstrong Siddeley landaulette limousine and the smartly dressed chauffeur. The vehicle was first registered in 1921. It was a 30hp model with a 4960cc engine. Despite much use of aluminium in construction it still weighed about two tons and performance was not particularly good with a maximum speed of around 65mph.*

DL 2294 *Also first registered in 1921 was this Star 18-seat charabanc. It was operated by H.P. Colenutt of Sandown as part of his fleet of around six charabancs which Colenutt ran under the trading name of "Star" until 1931. Several of the vehicles were actually produced by Star Engineering Company of Wolverhampton, a major manufacturer of cars and commercial vehicles until 1928 when taken over by Guy Motors, eventually going into liquidation in 1932.*

DL 2354 *This is an Overland four-seat tourer, manufactured in Indianapolis, USA and new in July 1921. The people are not known but the photograph appears to have been taken at a wedding, almost certainly on the Isle of Wight.*

DL 2371 *This solid-tyred Dennis three ton lorry was first registered on 13th July 1921. It is seen here at Calbourne Mill probably delivering grain to be ground into flour. The vehicle was owned by George Weeks and Son, who owned the water mill. In addition to its main duties of carrying grain and flour the lorry was regularly fitted with some temporary seats and used to take villagers shopping in Newport on Saturdays. George Weeks and Son held a Road Service Licence for this operation.*

DL 2387 *Unic one-and-a-half-ton van, first registered 26th July 1921 to Percy Reynolds, carrier of Ningwood. Mr Reynolds had been a carrier with a horse-drawn service from the Ningwood and Shalfleet areas to Newport for many years. DL 2387 was probably his earliest motorised vehicle.*

DL 2577 *Walter Lock inherited Elmsworth Farm, near Porchfield from his affluent father Robert in 1906. Walter's wife (in the rear seat of the car) was born Elizabeth Hayward, a farmer's daughter from nearby Locks Green. Walter was the first owner of such a handsome vehicle in the district as this Bullnose Morris tourer. Walter and his wife are pictured outside Elmsworth farmhouse around 1922.*

DL 4582 and DL 4584 *Several Morris vans and cars owned by Upward and Rich, Newport. In the 1920s Upward and Rich had a major grocer's shop in the centre of Newport. This photo shows their garage where they stored their delivery vehicles. Most Upward and Rich vehicles appeared to be manufactured by Morris at that time. DL 4582 was a Morris one-and-a-half-ton van which was first registered on 4th May 1926. DL 4584 was a 'Bullnose' Morris car.*

Vibrant scene at Cowes during a mid-1920s regatta week. *None of the vehicles has a DL registration number but this line up of vintage cars at Cowes Parade demanded inclusion. From left to right the makes are Austin, Bentley, Lea-Francis, Trojan, Morris and Morris.*

DL 5297 *Triumph 494cc motorcycle combination being ridden by Mr George Frederick Buckett (1880 – 1973) of Knighton, near Newchurch in 1968. First registered in 1927. The total price for the new motorcycle and sidecar including delivery from C.F. Stagg of Newport was £56. George Buckett, much loved grandfather of Shelagh Gaylard, worked for the water board for 73 years. Shelagh remembers one occasion as a girl when her grandfather drove her in the sidecar to the Newchurch Horticultural Show. As they reached the top of Newchurch Shute he accelerated and they went over the hill with a jump, almost causing Shelagh to drop the eggs and flowers she was carrying. George Buckett lived and worked at Knighton Water Works as a Superintendent and owned the bike until his death.*

DL 5769 *Keith Weeks, another member of the Calbourne Mill Weeks family, stands proudly in front of his first car – a Morris – which was new in 1928. The photograph was taken at Freshwater Causeway Bridge at the head of the Western Yar in 1949.*

DL 5854? *Francis Barnett solo motorcycle, c.150cc being ridden by Herbie Wheeler in Southern Vectis driver's uniform outside his home in Locks Green, Porchfield. Mr. Wheeler sold his bus service from Porchfield to Newport to Southern Vectis in 1935. As a condition of this business transaction Mr Wheeler was given a contract to work for that bus operator and he continued to drive buses for the company until the early 1950s with several awards for safe driving. Presumably Herbie Wheeler used this motorcycle for his daily journey to work to the Nelson Road bus garage in Newport.*

DL 6184 *This is a Douglas motorcycle ridden by William (Will) Mortram leading the St Helens carnival. This machine was first registered to E.W. Wade of St Helens in March 1929.*

DL 6314 *Ford Model A truck, first registered 4th May 1929. This attractive commercial vehicle was owned by W. Matthews and Sons, Newport, timber merchants and fencing contractors.*

DL 6358 *Sunbeam 500cc motorcycle, manufactured in 1929. Bert Buckett with his mother Hilda and pet dog were photographed in the Porchfield area on Bert's motorcycle on 3rd September 1939 – the first day of the Second World War. The original owner was Mr A.V. Richards of Ryde.*

DL 6369 *Ford Model AA refuse collection lorry. F.J. Rolf of Ventnor bought this Ford two-ton lorry new in the summer of 1929. The lengthened Ford Model AA commercial chassis could be fitted with a variety of bodies. Mr Rolf had a contract with Ventnor Urban District Council to collect rubbish in the town and this specialised commercial vehicle was manufactured solely for this purpose. Rubbish was loaded into the vehicle through lift up flaps and the lorry was emptied by handle-wound tipping gear. It was operated by Rolf for many years.*

DL 6477 *Ford Model AA one-and-a-half-ton ambulance, first registered 17th July 1929. This sturdy and well-proportioned vehicle was delivered new to British Red Cross Society, Newport. The driver and rural location are unknown.*

4 DL, ADL, BDL and CDL VEHICLES 1930 to 1939

In the late 1920s, following the growth of motor traffic and an increasing number of accidents, a Royal Commission on Transport was appointed. The Royal Commission issued a detailed report entitled "The Control of Traffic on Roads" in 1929. Under Transport Minister Herbert Morrison the Road Traffic Act 1930 was passed. This Act adopted virtually all of the recommendations contained in the Royal Commission's comprehensive report.

The main provisions relating to motor cars were:-

- Classification of motor vehicles
- Construction, weight and equipment regulations for motor vehicles
- Compulsory third party insurance
- Issue of the Highway Code
- Introduction of driving offences – dangerous, reckless and careless driving whilst being unfit and under the influence of drink or drugs
- The first UK driving tests (for disabled drivers only)
- Abolition of all speed limits for cars

The Act also introduced some very important changes for the increased regulation of bus and coach services. A regional network of Traffic Commissioners was established and these bodies became responsible for issuing route licences for new services. In addition the rules regarding the conduct of drivers, conductors and passengers were strengthened and limitations were imposed upon the hours of continuous driving. A 30mph speed limit was introduced for buses and coaches.

By the early 1930s new motor vehicles were becoming more technically advanced and were beginning to have much more rounded and streamlined bodies, a trend which would continue into the post-war years. Also the rate of introduction of new DL-registered vehicles carried on increasing. For example, DL 8014, a 20-seat Bedford WLB bus with Duple bodywork, was delivered new to Colson Brothers, Carisbrooke on 1st August 1932. DL 9015, a 20-seat Dennis Ace bus with Harrington bodywork (see photograph in Chapter 5), was delivered new to Southern Vectis on 14th June 1934. It was clear that a new numbering system would soon be required.

In keeping with many other parts of Britain the Isle of Wight changed from two-letter to three-letter local registration codes, after DL 9999 was issued on 10th October 1935. ADL 1 was issued on the same day to a vehicle owned by Sir S. Hanson Rowbotham of Brighstone. The make of this car which was supplied by Stratstone Ltd. in London is unknown, although it was probably prestigious.

Many of the 6,250 Isle of Wight registration numbers issued in the 1930s up to the outbreak of the Second World War in September 1939 were for buses, coaches and commercial vehicles. Car ownership levels in the county remained low and the vast majority of residents and visitors relied on the railways and local bus services to meet their everyday travel needs. There were also far more carriers and mobile shops than in recent years to meet the needs of the more rural communities.

Supported by high levels of funding from the Southern Railway, Southern Vectis rapidly acquired many of the other bus operators on the Isle of Wight and their established routes. In addition to obtaining some good quality second hand buses Southern Vectis invested in many new vehicles, virtually all of which carried DL registrations. Often the company reserved batches of distinctive number plates, a practice which was to continue for many years. Several examples during the 1930s were as follows: ten Dennis Lancet 36-seat buses (DL 9000 to 9009); six Dennis Ace 20-seat buses (DL 9010 to 9015); thirteen Dennis Lancets (DL 9700 to 9712); six Dennis Lance double deck buses (ADL 500 to 505); seven Bristol L5G 35-seat buses (BDL 850 to 856); a further sixteen Bristol L5Gs (CDL 600 to 615) and, rather strangely, a Bristol K5G double deck bus and two Dennis Falcon 20-seat buses (CDL 899 to 901).

A number of other firms followed this practice of reserving batches of DL registrations for their fleets of vehicles. In keeping with the relatively small population of the Island batches were normally not very large. Some other pre-war examples were as follows: Vectis Bus Company's first batch DL 2446 to 2448; Fowler's 'Royal Blue' Daimler coaches DL 3056 to 3058; Vectis Bus Company's largest batch in the 1920s DL 5576 to 5582;

Jolliffe Bothers (Coal Merchants) Ford lorries DL 6142 to 6151 and Fountain Garage, Cowes who purchased a fleet of five new Standard 12 saloons which it operated as taxis (CDL 617 to 621).

The complete series of 'CDL' registrations up to CDL 999 was issued prior to the start of the Second World War on 3rd September 1939. The only known exception is CDL 998 where the vehicle, a groundsman's tractor, was not registered until June 1940. Many motor vehicles were registered in August and September 1939. These included a small number of early 'DDL' registrations, as follows:

DDL 1 P.J. Duff, Sandown, supplied by himself, 1/9/1939
DDL 2 Mr Steadman, Sandown, supplied by P.J. Duff, 1/9/39
DDL 3 Cheek Brothers, Chale, supplied by Canning Day Ltd., Newport, 1/9/1939
DDL 5 Frank Cheverton Ltd., supplied by themselves, 1/9/1939
DDL 6 Fowlers Isle of Wight Ltd., Newport, supplied by themselves, 1/9/1939
DDL 7 Ball and Son, Cowes, supplied by Canning Day Ltd., 1/9/1939
DDL 8 A. Morey, Ryde, motorcycle supplied by C.F. Stagg, Newport, 1/9/1939
DDL 10 Capt. R. Carson, Bonchurch, supplied by G.K. Nash, Ventnor, 2/9/1939
DDL 11 Day, S. Canning, Binstead, supplied by Canning Day, Newport, 2/9/1935
DDL 12 Fowlers Isle of Wight Ltd., Newport, supplied by themselves, 2/9/1935

The remaining 'DDL' registrations were issued during the war and in the early part of 1946. These were mainly allocated to tractors, commercial vehicles and buses which were considered essential in maintaining food production, allowing local businesses to survive and enabling people to get to work.

This photograph shows the Smith and Whitehead garage at the junction of South Street and Church Litten, Newport in the 1930s. This site has been redeveloped. It became the Canning Day garage and is currently occupied by a Morrison's supermarket car park.

DL 7036 *Chevrolet 14-seat coach, new to F.C. Fanner, of Melville Street, Sandown on 26th March 1930. This photograph is believed to have been taken some time between 1934 and 1937 when the vehicle was sold. The 'garter' on the side of the coach bears the name I.W. Luxe Coaches and the monogram is F M T, standing for Fanner's Motor Tours.*

DL 7042 *'Flatnose' Morris. After several years of producing distinctive bullnose-radiator motor cars in the 1920s Morris switched to quite different vehicle designs. This Morris Oxford 6 was first registered in June 1930 to C.W.P. Branson who lived in Parkhurst.*

DL 7065 *Southern Vectis purchased thirteen new AEC Reliance 32-seat buses with Dodson dual entrance bodywork in 1930. They formed the backbone of the operator's fleet in the early 1930s. DL 7065 was photographed at Ryde Esplanade prior to departure on the short service to Seaview. The vehicle was withdrawn in 1938.*

DL 7515 *Dennis Arrow 28-seat coach with London Lorries bodywork. First registered on 5th June 1931 this coach was delivered new to H.G. Eames, Shanklin for excursions and private hire work. The vehicle passed into the ownership of Southern Vectis in 1937 and continued to see active service on the Island until June 1950. This photograph was taken at Ryde Esplanade in July 1949.*

DL 7594 *Hillman Wizard four-door saloon. This fine looking vehicle was first registered on 7th July 1931. It was delivered new to Mr A.J. Bartlett of East Cowes. A period advertisement from 1932 records that this vehicle would have cost £198 (chassis only) or £270 for a fully completed car.*

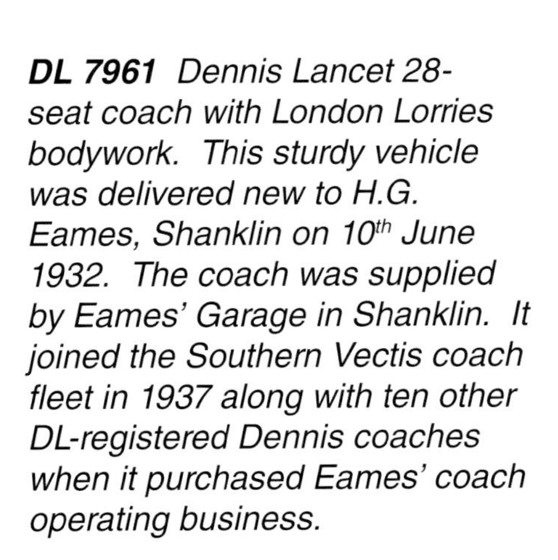

DL 7961 *Dennis Lancet 28-seat coach with London Lorries bodywork. This sturdy vehicle was delivered new to H.G. Eames, Shanklin on 10th June 1932. The coach was supplied by Eames' Garage in Shanklin. It joined the Southern Vectis coach fleet in 1937 along with ten other DL-registered Dennis coaches when it purchased Eames' coach operating business.*

DL 8279 *Ford Model 40. This was a rare Ford Model B with a V8 engine. It probably had a bespoke coachbuilt body. It must have been one of the earliest Fords to have had the V8 engine instead of the four cylinder one. The car was first registered on 4th February 1933 to Frank Cheverton in Brighstone, having been supplied by Frank Cheverton Ltd. in Newport.*

DL 8679 *Citroen. French motor cars were fairly uncommon on the Isle of Wight before the Second World War. This four door model, sporting the distinctive chevrons on the radiator, was supplied by Nash's Garage in Ventnor which had a Citroen dealership. It was first registered on* 4th *November 1933 and was owned by Mr Wearing who was the father of Roy Wearing and Fay Brown.*

DL 8711 *Austin Seven. This photograph shows Roy Wearing, the late brother of Fay Brown, with his first car - an Austin Seven coupe. The car was supplied by E.H. Crinage, Ventnor and it was first registered on* 1st *December 1933. When new the car was owned by Mr R.R. Earnshaw of Ventnor. Roy Wearing lived in Ventnor and edited the Isle of Wight Mercury local newspaper for many years. He passed away in 2004.*

DL 9001 *Dennis Lancet 36-seat bus with Eastern Counties bodywork. DL 9001 was one of a batch of ten rear-entrance Dennis Lancets which were delivered new to Southern Vectis in 1934. The photograph was taken outside the Isle of Wight County Club in St James Square, Newport. Note the bus conductor loading a passenger's bicycle onto the roof luggage rack. This must have been a fairly common occurrence at the time but one which was rarely recorded on film.*

DL 9086 *Leyland SKP3 dual purpose bus/ coach. This bus was delivered new to R. Walkden Ltd. (Walkden's Bus Service), Sandown in July 1934. It was used on Walkden's main route from Sandown to Ryde until 1936 when the firm was sold to Southern Vectis. The vehicle was fifteen years old when this photograph was taken in Sandown in July 1949.*

DL 9256 *Bedford shooting brake (estate car). This unusual vehicle was first registered on 1st October 1934. It probably accommodated about seven passengers and was useful for small group excursions. Herbie Wheeler is pictured standing by the driver's door, outside his home at Locks Green near Porchfield. The vehicle, which was supplied by Canning Day Ltd., was owned by Mr H.A. Wills, a Newport businessman.*

DL 9589 *Bedford 25cwt van. First registered on 1st April 1935 this sturdy commercial vehicle was supplied by Porter and Wootton and delivered new to Kingswells Dairy in Ventnor. It was operated by the firm for several years and must have been well suited to delivering milk to the many hotels, shops and private houses in this very hilly town. The driver is unknown.*

ADL 392 *Bedford WTB 20-seat bus with Duple bodywork, supplied by Canning Day Ltd.. This handsome vehicle was delivered new to Colson Brothers of Carisbrooke in May 1936 and it worked on their frequent service from Newport to Carisbrooke and Gunville. In 1939 the firm was sold to Southern Vectis. Two former Colson Bedford WTBs (ADL 392 and BDL 287) continued to operate on the same route for their new owner up to 1954. The photograph was taken in St James Square, Newport during the Second World War.*

BDL 307 *This Bedford WTB coach was first registered on 5th June 1937. It was supplied by Canning Day Ltd., Newport and was delivered to Bernard Groves of Cowes. Groves continued to operate excursions and private hire contracts until 1955 when the company was sold to Southern Vectis. The fleet at that time comprised three Bedford OB 29-seat coaches and a Bedford SB 33-seat coach. These vehicles carried the post-war Isle of Wight registration numbers EDL 808, FDL 240, GDL 102 and HDL 570. Bernard Groves' garage, where this photograph was taken, was superbly located at 'The Arcade', less than one minute's walk from the Red Funnel ferry terminal at West Cowes.*

BDL 734 *Ford V8 saloon. This powerful car was supplied by Frank Cheverton Ltd. and was first registered on 10th December 1937. It was owned by Donald (Don) Thomas of Whippingham in the 1950s when this photograph was taken.*

CDL 15 *Ariel 500cc motorcycle. First registered on 13th April 1938 and supplied by C.F. Stagg, Newport to Mr D.H. King of Merstone. Note the blackout mask on the headlight for this wartime photograph.*

CDL 502 *Sunbeam 500cc motorcycle combination. This machine was supplied by C.F. Stagg, Newport and was first registered on 1st January 1939. Its original owner was Mr C.P. Stroud who lived in East Cowes.*

CDL 603 *Bristol L5G bus with Harrington bodywork, photographed at Ryde Esplanade. CDL 603 was one of a large batch of sixteen Bristol L5G 35-seat single deck buses to enter service with Southern Vectis in September 1939. CDL 600 to 613 had Harrington bodywork. CDL 614 and CDL 615 had bodywork designed by Eastern Counties and built in Newport by Harry Margham and Sons.*

BDL 101 *In 1937 Southern Vectis took delivery of a pair of Bristol GO5G 56-seat highbridge double deck buses with Eastern Coachworks bodywork (BDL 100 and BDL 101). This pre-war photograph shows BDL 101 at Ryde Esplanade. The vehicle was rebuilt from highbridge to lowbridge layout with major modifications in 1951 before being sold just three years later.*

CDL 998 *This Ford groundsman's tractor was supplied by Frank Cheverton Ltd., Newport. It was first registered on 11th June 1940 to Mr. R.J. Flux of Shalfleet. The vehicle still exists and was photographed at a Northwood Show in July 1975.*

DL-1222
DL-2218
DL 3304

SINGER
DL-3 609
DL 4405
DL
8773

5 SURVIVING PRE-WAR DL-REGISTERED VEHICLES

The prime focus of this book is on period images of pre-war DL-registered vehicles. Approximately 14,000 such vehicles existed for different lengths of time in the years from 1904 to 1939. Remarkably there are 117 known or likely 'survivors' all of which are over 75 years old. Brief details of each survivor are contained in Appendix 1. This list has been produced with assistance from several historic vehicle enthusiasts, especially Colin Thomas, John Golding, John Gregory and Don Vincent. It is not totally comprehensive and is subject to change (e.g. with regard to ownership and condition). The author would welcome any additional information, especially with regard to pre-war motorcycles which are thought to be under-recorded.

This chapter provides a colour photo gallery of twenty seven of these survivors and contains detailed histories of ten specific vehicles. A few of the vintage cars may be viewed in museums, including the National Motor Museum at Beaulieu in Hampshire. The majority are privately owned and may sometimes be seen on display at special events such as the annual Isle of Wight Steam Show at Havenstreet, the Isle of Wight Bus and Coach Museum's running days, the Isle of Wight County Show, the Garlic Festival, village fetes and carnivals. Around 35% are based on the Island, 60% on the mainland and 5% in other countries. There are a number of clubs which organise regular local events for their members. They include the Vectis Historic Vehicle Club, Isle of Wight Austins and the Morris Owners' Club.

A small number of these veteran and vintage motor vehicles have been kept in good running order since new. The vast majority have been restored at some stage during the past sixty years. Some have been kept under cover since they were used regularly and others have been rescued in derelict condition from exposed outdoor locations. Over the years most of the vehicles have changed hands several times. In a few cases, however, vehicles have remained in single ownership (e.g. Bristol K5G double deck bus CDL 899) or with several generations of the same family (e.g. ABC Skootamota DL 1930).

Many firms, individuals and organisations have been actively involved in the restoration, preservation, display and use of vintage Isle of Wight vehicles since the 1950s. Often commercial garages have had a major role to play in this process – sometimes storing very old cars and motorcycles at the back of a workshop or in a yard for several years until resources have become available to restore them to their former glory. Some of the key people who have conserved this part of the Island's economic and social heritage are the late Norman Ball, the late Rex Watson, the late Den Phillips, the late John Richie, the late Ernie Taylor, the Cheverton family, Bob Stay, Tim Day, John Golding, Geoff Golding, Barry Price, Ken Taylor, Derek Hunt, Derek Priddle, Colin Thomas and John Woodhams.

From the 1970s to the 1990s there were several excellent museums on the Isle of Wight which contained some fine vintage motor vehicles and traction engines with 'DL' registration numbers. The Norman Ball transport collection (which also included many horse-drawn vehicles and bicycles) was a nationally important museum, based at Westridge, near Ryde. This collection was dispersed at a Sotheby's auction in April 1991. The Isle of Wight Council's Heritage Museum at Westridge and the Albany Steam Museum at Newport both contained several pre-war motor vehicles but these have also closed as tourist attractions. The Isle of Wight Bus and Coach Museum contains many DL-registered public service vehicles but nearly all of them were built after the Second World War. Seven pre-war buses, charabancs and coaches with DL registrations are known to have survived. Only three of these vehicles (Dennis Ace bus DL 9015, Bedford WTB coach CDL 792 and Bristol K5G open top double deck bus CDL 899) are currently in good running order. The other four are all long term restoration projects, one of which (Dennis Lancet bus DL 9706) is fairly close to successful completion.

Finally, looking to the future, several owners of restored pre-war motor vehicles on the Isle of Wight are exploring the options for safeguarding and enhancing this important part of the Island's heritage/ local history for the benefit of future generations. There are a number of fascinating old cars, motorcycles, traction engines and commercial vehicles in private collections which could form the basis of a first class new tourist attraction. A well designed and suitably located museum, ideally managed by a trust of vintage vehicle enthusiasts and transport historians, would be a real asset to the Island's economy. It would complement the Isle of Wight Steam Railway and Isle of Wight Bus and Coach Museum. Such a museum could house a broad range of significant pre-war and immediate post-war vehicles and motoring memorabilia. In addition it could contain a restoration workshop with the potential for older enthusiasts to share their extensive knowledge and technical skills with younger people. This innovative type of museum could possibly become the venue for a number of special motoring exhibitions, shows and events to add to the diversity of the Island's rich social calendar. It is the author's sincere hope that this very positive vision will lead to the creation of an Isle of Wight Historic Motoring Museum which could be an excellent example of sustainable development.

__DL 33__ Benz 8hp 3-speed dogcart of 1898, manufactured by Benz et Cie., Mannheim, Germany. The vehicle had a two-cylinder engine of 1570cc. Despite its belt drive and archaic appearance the Benz was remarkably reliable for its day. This veteran car is believed to be the oldest surviving motor vehicle with its original Isle of Wight DL registration number which was probably issued in 1904. Little is known of the history of this very early motor car. It was displayed at the National Motor Museum at Beaulieu in the 1960s and is currently owned by the Daimler-Benz motor museum in Germany.

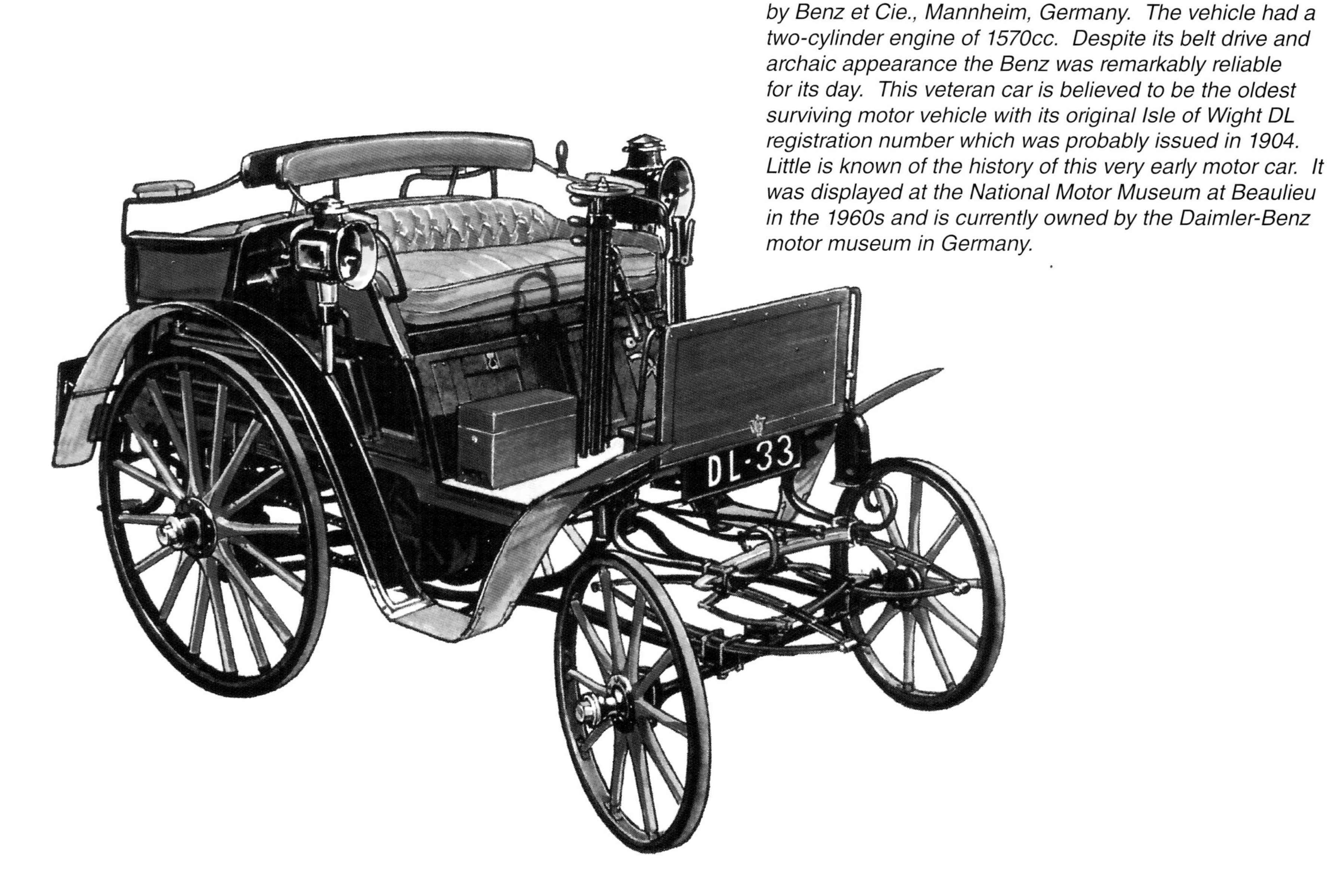

DL 74 *Clement 14hp four-cylinder car with open wagonette coachwork, 1903. The three photographs show the vehicle in use as a farmer's truck around 1925, shortly after being rescued as a derelict chassis around 1965 and completing the Veteran Car Club's London to Brighton Run around 1980.*

DL 74 is a Clement type AC4R manufactured by A. Clement, Levallois, Paris, France. When it was built in 1903 it did not require a registration number. Shortly after the Motor Car Act of 1903 came into force on 1st January 1904 the Clement became DL 74. This registration was retained under the Roads Act of 1920 which came into force on 1st January 1921.

The first and additional owners of the vehicle (if any) before 1920 are not known. By early 1920 the car was owned by a Mr. Moore of East Cowes. It was sold at that time to a Mr. G.E. Morris of Castle Farm, East Cowes for the sum of £50. Mr. Morris then removed the rear part of the wagonette body and replaced it with a load deck to make the vehicle suitable for his milk round and other farm uses. At the same time the engine was overhauled. The vehicle continued in this use until about 1927 or 1928, by which time it was almost 25 years old. Mr. Morris then purchased a Rover 8 and the Clement was laid up in a shed at his farm. The registration was officially cancelled on 5th October 1933.

In 1938, when Mr Morris moved to Woodhouse Farm, Whippingham DL 74, still laid up in its shed, was taken by Frank Cheverton in part exchange for a Fordson tractor. Frank Cheverton and Sons Ltd. were major motor suppliers and repairers, with premises in Lugley Street, Newport and elsewhere in the town. They were also agricultural engineers. Chevertons had some interest in historic vehicles and had set aside a collection of interesting cars – some complete and mobile and some in need of rebuilding. For some time the Clement and an Alldays and Onions of similar age were kept in part of the agricultural yard adjoining the river Medina and partly below the brick arches of the viaduct carrying the Isle of Wight Central Railway line as it headed south from Newport Station towards Shide. It is understood that the area was liable to flooding and both cars were partially submerged more than once. Many parts had been stolen or lost from both cars over the 1939 to 1945 period and they became virtually derelict. Prior to the major roadworks and development, including the removal of the railway line, which took place in this part of Newport around 1960 the cars were moved to Gunville Brickworks. This site, on the western outskirts of Newport, was owned by the Cheverton business.

In the summer of 1964 the presence of the cars became known to John Golding and the late Rex Watson. Both vehicles were, by then, virtually hidden from view in dense undergrowth and brambles. An approach was then made to Frank Cheverton who advised that the cars were now so derelict that he could not contemplate reconstruction. Following discussions, the Clement passed to John Golding and the Alldays and Onions passed to Rex Watson. DL 74 was collected from Gunville on 24th October 1964 and taken to John Golding's premises in Wellow, Isle of Wight.

Some research into the history of DL 74 was done. On 8th November 1976 the unrestored car was passed to Roland Frayne of Naas, County Kildare, Eire. Mr. Frayne was much involved with early motor vehicles and had the knowledge and facilities to totally rebuild the car. It was agreed that, if possible, the original DL 74 registration would remain with the Clement. The restoration progressed well. Just four years after leaving the Isle of Wight as a total wreck the vehicle returned to the UK to take part, successfully, in the Veteran Car Club's London to Brighton Run on 2nd November 1980. It is known to have completed the London to Brighton Run several times since then. This miraculous survivor passed to Johnny Thomas of Carmarthen, South Wales in 2003/2004. It is now over 110 years old.

DL 126 *Rover 6hp car, 1906. This beautiful little two-seater is still in excellent running condition and is currently owned by Tim Day on the Isle of Wight. It has spent much of its life on the mainland in the East Midlands. It was owned for many years by Mr. P.H. Pointer. A meticulous restoration of the car was carried out for him by David Bliss. The vehicle passed to Mr Bliss around 1990 and he carried out some further enhancements and took the car to various shows and rallies. Tim Day returned this superb vehicle to the Island, complete with wooden framed wheels, in 2011. It was one of the stars of the Isle of Wight Steam Show at Havenstreet in August 2013.*

DL 259 *Itala 120hp two-seat racing car, 1907. This famous vehicle was built by Fabbrica Automobili Itala in Torino, Italy with a huge four-cylinder engine of 14432cc to qualify for the 1907 French Grand Prix. It did not compete in this race, however, probably because it was not ready in time. Two months later it was entered for the "Coppa del Velocita" race in Bresica, an event for Grand Prix cars, and was driven to a magnificent win by top Italian driver Alessandro Cagno. Despite a ten minute delay at the start with a faulty magneto Cagno worked his Itala through the entire field on a twisting course to win the race in brilliant style, at an average speed of 62.5mph. The car was obsolete in 1908 due to a change in regulations and it was sold. It was later purchased by Mrs. Edgar Thornton and was issued with Isle of Wight registration number DL 259. This remarkable car was driven on the Island and mainland in touring trim by Mrs Thornton and her husband until 1931 when it was stored. The car was left in Mrs Thornton's will to Frank Cheverton. Subsequently the Itala was loaned to and restored by the National Motor Museum at Beaulieu, where it is often displayed.*

DL 821 *Vauxhall C type "Prince Henry" 25hp four-speed tourer, 1913. The Vauxhall Prince Henry was renowned for its speed, flexibility and good roadholding and some models were raced successfully by the company. This superb car was built by Vauxhall Motors, Luton, and had a four-cylinder engine of 3969cc. The car was purchased new by the late Mrs. F.A. Cheverton and laid up in 1923 after it had only covered 15,000 miles. In the late 1950s Frank Cheverton asked his skilled motor engineer Bob Stay to restore the vehicle which had been 'mothballed' in a private garage for many years. Following a very successful restoration the vehicle was loaned by Mr. Cheverton to the National Motor Museum where it is still located.*

DL 1081 *Alldays and Onions motorcycle, c.1912. Alldays and Onions of Birmingham was a very long-established company with its roots in the seventeenth century. During the nineteenth century they manufactured bicycles and built their first powered tricycle in 1898 with a de Dion engine. Alldays and Onions started producing their own motorcycle engines from 1903. They also manufactured cars and tractors. This particular motorcycle is believed to have been built around 1912. It is currently owned by Mr. Case on the Isle of Wight.*

DL 1930 *ABC Skootamota, c.1919. This 125cc motorcycle was manufactured at Somerton, near Cowes. Having been in the ownership of the same family since new, DL 1930 was expertly restored on the Isle of Wight by Mr. George Davis between 2003 and 2005.*

DL 1930 *ABC Skootamota DL 1930 was bought new in 1919 by Albert Edward Young of Totland, Isle of Wight when he was about forty years old. It is shown in the top photograph being ridden by his daughter, Mrs. Day, the mother of Mrs Jeanette Davis in 1940. When Mr Young died the Skootamota was left to his son who lived in Netley, near Southampton. The Skootamota was stored in a garden shed for many years until Mr Young's son passed away. The disused vehicle was then given to Mr Young's granddaughter, Jeanette Davis, who lived on the Isle of Wight with her husband George Davis. George was a retired mechanical engineering instructor for the armed forces. Between 2003 and 2005 George carried out a thorough restoration of this rare vintage vehicle which had been built at Somerton on the Island. As it approaches its centenary this pioneer motor scooter is back in full working order and is sometimes displayed at local shows by its proud owners.*

STAG LANE
MOTORS
522443
DL 2218

DL 2108 *Marshall 6hp traction engine "Faithfull", 1909. This attractive traction engine has spent virtually all of its life on the Isle of Wight. It was originally owned by Mr. A. Faithfull of Barnsley Farm, Ryde and was first registered for road use as DL 2108 in 1921. The iconic vehicle was restored at the Albany Steam Museum, Newport and owned by Ken Taylor. He sold it to Bob Stay who also owned this special vehicle for a number of years and displayed it at many local shows. It is currently owned by the Jenkins family. The late Mrs. Connie Jenkins was Mr. Faithfull's daughter so the traction engine has returned to its original family.*

DL 2218 *Ford Model TT two-ton truck. This sturdy lorry was delivered new to H.P. Colenutt, Sandown in 1921. Its main use was probably as a breakdown vehicle for Mr. Colenutt's Broadway Garage and fleet of 'Star' charabancs in the 1920s. DL 2218 was acquired by Bob Stay and restored by him to pristine condition. It has attended many local shows over the past 40 years and has provided excellent publicity for Mr. Stay's business, Stag Lane Motors.*

DL 2151

DL 2151 *Alldays and Onions tractor, built c.1918 and first registered in 1921. This rare early tractor was purchased in semi-derelict condition for £1 and a dozen eggs by the late Mr. Den Phillips of Compton Farm near Freshwater Bay. Mr Phillips carried out a full restoration of the tractor and displayed it at many shows and local fetes before it was sold at an auction of historic vehicles for a considerably higher sum.*

DL 2610 *Leyland C1 26-seat charabanc, "Red Chief", new to G.K. Nash, Ventnor in 1922. This rare vehicle is being completely rebuilt and restored by its current owner Geoff Golding. After several years of painstaking work the chassis has been fully restored and fitted with a new set of solid rubber tyres. The engine has been overhauled and is in working order. The final major part of this ambitious long-term project is the construction of an authentic replacement charabanc body with folding hood.*

History of Leyland 23-seat charabanc DL 2610

On 30th March 1922 this Leyland charabanc was delivered new to G.K. Nash, 23 Pier Street, Ventnor, supplied via Turner and Blakeway of Southampton for a total cost of £1271. The vehicle comprised a Leyland C1 chassis with four-cylinder petrol engine, all running units, solid-tyred wheels and Leyland-built 23-seat open coachwork with hood. This was Gerry Nash's first charabanc and was painted in a red and black livery. It was named "Red Chief" following Mrs Nash's suggestion that her husband's coaches should be named after characters in the epic poem "The Song of Hiawatha". The charabanc was used extensively for excursions and 'Round the Island' tours. It was upgraded to pneumatic tyres around 1926 and continued in use until withdrawn in 1931 or 1932.

It was then sold to Mr F Cheek – farmer, contractor and haulier – of Chale Abbey Farm, near Ventnor. The charabanc body was removed (the seats finding a new life in a café) and a lorry cab and drop-side body was made and fitted. The Leyland then did a lot of heavy work hauling chalk from a quarry for use in the construction of the Yaverland to Sandown embankment. Subsequently the lorry bed was removed and the chassis was fitted with a donkey-engine driven stone crusher. One half-shaft was removed to facilitate towing and it was thus moved from site to site until ending up, disused, in the quarry at St. George's Down, Blackwater, Newport which was operated by Cheek Brothers. The stone crusher was removed, but in so doing it was raised and then dropped causing damage to the chassis and torque tube. It is understood that the chassis had been sold to a scrap dealer early in the Second World War, along with several other former coaches then being used as lorries within the quarry. The abandoned vehicle was never collected, however, due to it having been left in an inaccessible part of the quarry.

In June 1964 the 'remains' of the vehicle (chassis, mechanical units and part of the lorry cab) passed to John Golding. The removal from its location in the quarry was difficult. Transport by road was by a heavy 'recovery ambulance' under the front axle, and on its own rear wheels, pulled by 1931 REO 'Speed Wagon' truck DL 7564 (see photo of this other survivor later in chapter 5). The vehicle passed to John's brother Geoff Golding in 1981 and initial restoration work started. Currently, after an enormous amount of meticulous work where every component had to be stripped, repaired and rebuilt, it is a running chassis, capable of moving under its own power. It has now reverted to original type wheels with solid tyres and the dash-panel has been reformed to charabanc profile. The chassis has been painted black with red wheels. Geoff Golding is now giving consideration to the construction of a replica charabanc body. Hopefully one day this astonishing survivor DL 2610 will be fully restored to its former glory as an Isle of Wight charabanc from the 1920s.

DL 3233 *1923 Rover 8 coupe, powered by an 1130cc air cooled flat twin engine. Supplied new on 30th July 1923 by Arthur Holmes' garage in Cowes, the car seems to have spent most of its life in Scotland and the north of England. It first appeared in a clearance auction by Metcalf's, scrap car dealers in Darlington. Next it was recorded as lot 22 in the 1962 sale of the Sword collection in Scotland when it moved to North Yorkshire. After a short spell in Kent and an appearance at the Manchester classic car show it became lot 19 at the 1983 Beaulieu auction, whereupon it disappeared for twenty years. The ninety year old car showed up again recently at an auction in Buxton and was then purchased by Mr. Colin Thomas from a Gloucestershire classic car dealer. This rare car is one of around 50 surviving Rover 8s, only three of which are coupes. It is back on the Isle of Wight in first class running order after many years on the mainland.*

The two photographs of DL 3233 on the facing page were taken outside the same house in Westhill Road, Cowes. The upper photo was taken in the mid-1920s on the occasion of a Cowes carnival, when the Rover was almost new. The lower photo was taken by the car's current owner around 2012.

ANCIENT
AND
MODERN
Roslin

DL 3233

DL 3304 *Ford Model T 15cwt van, first registered on 11th October 1923. The last registered owner prior to restoration was Mr. J. Cassell of Shorwell. This small commercial vehicle has been owned by Mr Bob Stay since the mid-1950s. After carrying out an immaculate restoration, Bob Stay has entered his Model T van in many historic vehicle rallies and shows on the Island and mainland, winning several "best in class" and "best in show" awards.*

Bob Stay discovered DL 3304 at Shorwell, still with its first owner Mr J. Cassell. It was being used as a chicken house. Apart from some superficial damage the vehicle was found to be complete and in fairly sound condition with a low mileage. The bodywork had been constructed by Harry Margham in Newport and was "plate-built and mouseproof". Having agreed a price of £2 with the farmer Bob loaded the van onto a trailer and towed it back to his home. He spent the next couple of years carrying out a complete restoration of the vehicle in the open air including a full overhaul of the engine. Bob's father-in-law was very fond of Ford Model Ts and helped him with this 'evenings and weekends' project. During the project Bob needed to get the vehicle professionally repainted and asked Reg Cheverton how much he would charge to paint a Ford Model T. Reg Cheverton replied "If you really own a Ford Model T the company will paint it for nothing." Imagine his amazement when Bob drove the vehicle into the garage! Chevertons kept their promise to paint the vehicle free of charge, on condition that it carried their name on the sides for free publicity.

When he had completed the restoration to his satisfaction Bob's first major trip was to the Historic Commercial Vehicle Club's inaugural rally at Beaulieu in 1957. Much to his delight he was awarded the "best in rally" prize. Shortly afterwards the vehicle was driven to Southall, West London for another major rally at the former AEC factory. Again DL 3304 was awarded the "best in rally" prize, which was presented with Lord Brabazon in attendance.

Further success followed at the Model T Register inaugural event at Beaulieu when the van was awarded the prize of "best commercial vehicle in the rally".

For some years Bob Stay allowed the vehicle to be stored at Chevertons' showroom in central Newport. When Chevertons was taken over by Premier Motors in the 1980s the new owners thought that the vehicle was part of the acquisition and removed it to the mainland. As soon as he heard about this situation Bob Stay immediately drove to the Premier Motors' depot, explained that he was the legal owner of DL 3304 and brought it back to the Island on a low-loader lorry. Since then the vehicle has been a popular visitor to many Isle of Wight County Shows and special transport events.

SINGER
DL-3 609

SINGER
DL-3 609

SINGER
DL-3 609

DL 3609 is a rare Singer 10 two-seat tourer with dickey seat. This was Bob Stay's next restoration project when he had restored DL 3304. DL 3609 was new in 1924 and its first owner was Mr Hayles, a Newport butcher. After some years Mr Hayles sold the Singer car to his Uncle, Mr Ash who lived in Newtown. It had fallen into disrepair and had been laid up for some years in Mr Ash's garage at the bottom of his garden. Hearing about this pre-war Isle of Wight vehicle Bob Stay contacted Mr Ash via a friend in Newtown but was informed that "the vehicle was not for sale and that he was intending to get it back on the road".

Within a year Mr Ash passed away. Bob Stay was introduced to Mr Ash's niece and her mother (who remembered being driven in the car when she was a young woman). They decided that Bob could take the car and related spare parts for nothing if he promised to restore the vehicle to its former glory and to take them for a ride in the car when it was back on the road. The vehicle had been partly dismantled but Bob managed to find all the components including the carburettor which was in a different part of the garage.

The vehicle was stored for several years inside an old Ronsons' van. Restoration work started when convenient and in due course it was completed to a very high standard. Bob Stay then contacted the elderly relative of the late Mr Ash and invited her out for lunch. She was absolutely delighted to be taken to and from the restaurant in the vintage Singer. During the past thirty years the vehicle has been displayed at a number of Isle of Wight County Shows and village fetes and has attracted many favourable comments. The little Singer is still in excellent condition for a ninety year old car.

DL 4405 *Bullnose Morris four-seat tourer, first registered in 1926. This handsome car was probably new to Sir John Simeon of Swainston Manor. It was rescued from Swainston by the late John Richie after it had been laid up in a barn for many years. Later it was purchased by Bob Stay from Whitwell around 1980. With the assistance of Alf McDine, Barry Carter and Norman Fish, Bob Stay carried out another first class restoration of a pre-war Isle of Wight car. The vehicle was in fair condition when obtained but needed a lot of work to return it to very good roadworthy condition.*

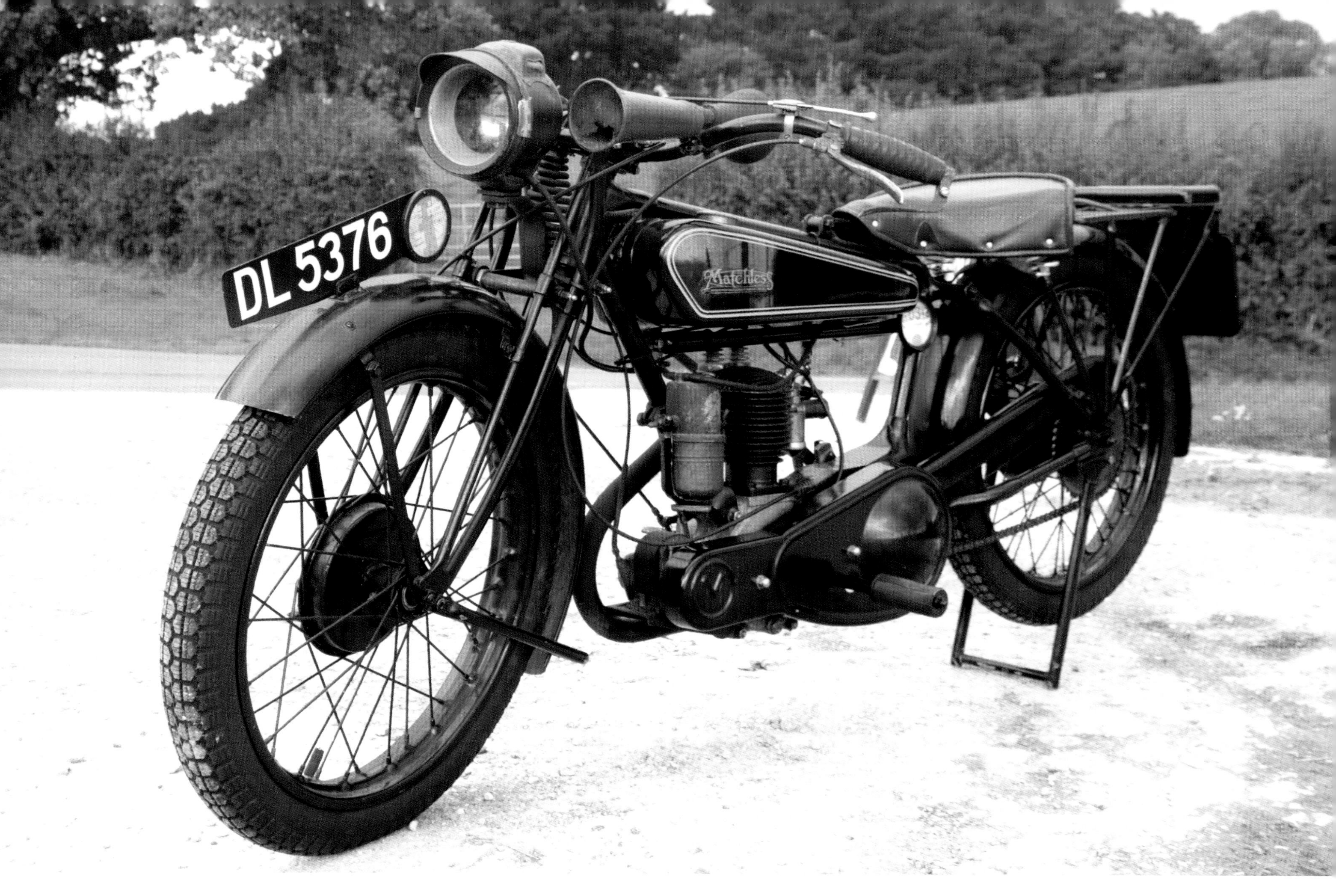

DL 5376 *Matchless Model R de luxe motorcycle. This motorcycle, which has a 250cc sidevalve engine, was first registered in 1927 to Mr. L. Harvey of Wroxall. At some stage it passed into the ownership of a café owner in Shanklin who was storing it in his shed. In 1976 Terry and Brian Chiverton heard about the old motorcycle from the owner who was a friend of Brian's. A few years later the brothers purchased the Matchless and stripped it down with a view to restoring it. Unfortunately work and family commitments prevented this plan. Some initial work was done but then the bike was stored carefully in Terry's garage. The motorcycle was advertised in the IW County Press in 2007 and Mr. John McConnell was the lucky buyer. It only took a few weeks to assemble the bike and the engine started on the first kick! "Violet", as she is known, is still being ridden by John McConnell on Island roads with original DL 5376 number plates, almost ninety years after she was manufactured.*

DL 5478 *Sentinel steam wagon. Delivered new to Westmore (Newport, IW) Ltd. in 1927. It was sold to H.B. Jolliffe, Cowes in 1945. The scarce vehicle somehow avoided being cut up for twenty years. It was fully restored in the 1970s by a group of vintage vehicle enthusiasts following a rescue from Mr. Jolliffe's scrapyard. It is currently in good working order and is displayed at various steam shows and rallies in East Anglia by its current owners.*

DL 7564 *REO truck, first registered on 1st July 1931 to Burt and Co., the Brewery, Ventnor. This rare commercial vehicle is currently being restored by John Golding on the Isle of Wight. It is expected that DL 7564 will be running on Island roads again in 2015.*

The chassis and all mechanical parts for DL 7564, including front wings, radiator, bonnet and scuttle, were manufactured by REO Motor Car Co. Inc. of Lansing, Michigan, USA. The vehicle was sent to the UK in 'knocked down' component form, and assembled by REO Motors (Britain) Ltd. at their works in Beavor Lane, Hammersmith, London W6 in 1931. The London works produced many hundred running chassis, of various models, for bodying by British coachbuilders. The chassis supplied is a type DF, a "Speed Wagon Super Tonner", a relatively light commercial vehicle with a twin-wheeled back axle. The engine is REO's own 'Gold Crown' six cylinder side valve petrol unit of 4400cc, with block cast in chrome nickel – publicised as being seven times harder than cast iron. It has a four speed manual gearbox and was readily capable of 65m.p.h.

The running chassis was supplied to the order of Burt and Co., the Brewery, High Street, Ventnor, through the Isle of Wight REO agent G.K. Nash, Motor Engineers, of Pier Street, Ventnor. It was sent to Harry Margham and Sons Ltd., Coachbuilders, of Crocker Street, Newport for bodywork which comprised a two-seat wooden framed cab and approximately nine foot flat bed timber load area with very short tailboard. The completed lorry was painted dark green, with red chassis, and was fully signwritten. It is thought to have replaced a 1921 Ford Model T lorry (DL 2191) in the brewery fleet. Apart from delivering beer, etc. to Burt's public houses around the Island, the lorry took part in various carnivals, including the 1938 Ventnor carnival where it appeared as 'Butterfly Fantasy'.

In August 1947 the REO retired from the brewery fleet, being replaced by a new Commer (EDL 986). It passed back to Nash's Garage and an 'in house' use was found for it as a recovery truck to retrieve broken down vehicles. The body and chassis beyond the back axle rearmost spring hanger were cut off and a crane and twin hooks were added. The "Speed Wagon" then settled down to a slower but quite strenuous new life which would last for the next fifteen years. Towing cars and commercial vehicles around hilly Ventnor was never easy and caused considerable wear and stress to certain mechanical units. It is a tribute to the quality of REO products that the lorry was still earning its keep when over thirty years old. It is worth noting that the firm of G.K. Nash also supplied REO vehicles to other owners on the Island. In addition they operated a fleet of coaches up to 1956 which had included at least four REO vehicles before the Second World War.

In July 1963 the lorry – devoid of crane – passed to the late Mr. Rex Watson, an historic vehicle enthusiast, and he used it for several years as his daily transport in the Yarmouth area. More exacting excursions included participation in the Historic Commercial Vehicle Club's London to Brighton Run in 1964. The old lorry continued to be used until 1980 when it was laid up on a rather insecure site at Wootton.

Historic vehicle enthusiast John Golding was aware of the situation and the lorry was towed to his premises at Wellow for 'safe storage'. Regrettably Rex Watson was unable to retain the lorry and it passed into John Golding's ownership in 1982. In 1988 the lorry was completely dismantled and stored. Pressure of work and other commitments delayed restoration until late 2011 but progress since then on replacing and reconditioning various mechanical components has been major. DL 7564 is now a rolling chassis again and will hopefully be fully restored and back on Island roads by 2015.

DL 7634 *Ford Model AA truck. Supplied by Frank Cheverton, Newport. Delivered new to Mr. W. Downer, Builder, Totland on 12th August 1931. Owned by Geoff Golding on the Isle of Wight since 1967. This stylish commercial vehicle is currently undergoing its second full restoration which will hopefully be completed in 2015. It should then be fit for another thirty years of active service.*

History of Ford Model A one-ton van DL 7994 (chassis number AF4791353)

From the factory the van went to Frank Cheverton Limited, Newport, the main Ford dealer on the Isle of Wight. It was first registered on 1st July 1932 to David Bridger-Sage, a market gardener. Mr. Bridger-Sage used the van as a mobile shop to sell the produce he had grown. The next known owner was Mr. William (Bill) Allam of Grange Farm, Wootton, who bought the van in August 1951. Mr. Allam was a dairy farmer and he used the van in connection with his business, mainly for delivering churns of fresh milk to the dairy. The above photograph shows Bill Allam's stepdaughter Janice Smith (nee Brinton) in front of DL 7994 at Grange Farm in 1951, when she was five years old.

In May 1956 a Mr. Wilfred James Montague from Lushington Hill, Wootton bought the van. Mr. Montague kept pigs and used the van to collect unwanted and leftover food (swill) to feed his animals. One of the main places he collected swill from was HM Prison at Parkhurst. The van was sold again in 1960 for £10 to a fourteen year old boy called Ron Long of Westwood Farm. Ron bought the van to drive around his father's farm. After about four years Ron parked the van in their Dutch barn and left it there. The van remained in the barn for about twelve years during which time the engine seized up, the tyres went flat and the vehicle generally deteriorated.

Around 1975/ 1976 Michael Maskell from Cowes spotted the van and bought it out of the barn for £125. He then renovated it and took it to local shows on the Island. The following photograph was taken in the late 1970s when the van was on display at an Isle of Wight County Show at Northwood.

In 1980 when it was just under fifty years old DL 7994 left the Isle of Wight when it was sold to a Michael John Smith of Steeple Clayton in Buckinghamshire. The van was later purchased by a Mr. David Hallam of Buxton, Derbyshire in 1988.

The current owner bought the van from Mr. Hallam in 1999. He has carried out some high quality restoration work and converted the vehicle into a mobile fruit and fish sales van. The firm named on the side of the van was started in 1921 by the owner's grandfather and is still in existence in 2014. In 1921 the firm had a Ford Model T van painted in the same smart livery and with a similar sign on the side.

DL 8773 *Ford Model Y coupe with unusual Salmons and Sons coachwork. This very rare Cairn 'Tickford' drop-head coupe version was supplied by Frank Cheverton, Newport on 3rd January 1934. It was one of only two such vehicles to be registered on the Isle of Wight. Its first Isle of Wight owner was Mr Hayles of Newport (who sold Singer DL 3609 to his uncle when he bought the beautiful Model Y coupe). It was restored by Mr. Bob Stay and was driven by Mrs. Stay on the Isle of Wight for many years. The vehicle was entered for the Queen's Silver Jubilee Parade at Windsor Castle in 1977 and won the concours d'elegance award. This vintage car has a recorded mileage of 31,000 miles and remains in very good running order.*

DL 8961 *Austin 10 four-door saloon. Supplied by G.K. Nash, Ventnor it was first registered to Miss A. Penfold of Ventnor on 17th April 1934. This vehicle was owned by the Ball family from around 1960 and was part of the Norman Ball transport collection at Westridge, Ryde up to 1991. It is still in use and may sometimes be seen at car rallies on the mainland.*

DL 9015 *Dennis Ace 20-seat bus with Harrington bodywork. This small hardworking vehicle was one of a batch of six Dennis Aces delivered new to Southern Vectis in 1934 for service on rural routes (DL 9010 to 9015). It was ideally suited to the Island's narrow country lanes and was operated by the company for 25 years before being sold to Medina Camps (IW) Ltd. After being laid up for many years the bus has been wonderfully restored to its original condition, complete with its pre-war livery, by Derek Priddle of Farnham. It is pictured at the Isle of Wight Bus and Coach Museum's Running Day at Newport Quay in October 2010.*

DL 9081 *Austin 7 RP box saloon. The Austin 7 was a reliable and economical small family car. Several different models were produced at Longbridge from 1922 to 1939 in very large numbers. It played a major role in making motoring affordable for people in the UK on average incomes. DL 9081 was supplied by Frank Cheverton, Newport and was first registered to Mr. S.A. Fenn of East Cowes on 11th June 1934. It is currently owned by Mr. Tony Hayter on the Isle of Wight and may sometimes be seen at local historic vehicle events.*

ADL 962 *Austin 10/4 6/8 cwt light delivery van. Supplied by Frank Cheverton, Newport to Mr. G. Lower, Newport on 1st January 1937. ADL 962 is one of around 30 survivors of 15,000 made. Two of the vehicle's early owners were Coleman's Pork Butchers of Regent Street, Shanklin and A.J. Mew, Butchers of Shanklin High Street. The next owner was Mr. R. Gallop a general builder of Wroxall. The vehicle was abandoned in Mr. Gallop's yard along with another in the 1960s. It was bought by the late John Richie in the late 1960s, "repaired" and put to work in his car spares business.*

Later the vehicle was sold to Mr. Ken Taylor of the Albany Steam Museum until sale to a Mr. Hibbard of Doncaster. Next it was used in an antiques business in Lancashire by Mr. Keith Pearson and it ended up at auction in 1981 worn out and with a bent axle. ADL 962 was purchased by Mr. Phil Taylor and put back on the road sixteen years later and after 54,000 miles was sold to Colin Thomas in 2009 who returned her to the Isle of Wight. The vehicle is in very good running order and attends many events of the Vectis Historic Vehicle Club and Isle of Wight Austins.

CDL 792 *Bedford WTB 26-seat coach with Duple Hendonian bodywork. Supplied by Canning Day, Newport to Shotters of Brighstone on 1st June 1939. This beautifully preserved public service vehicle is owned by Mr. John Woodhams, who operates vintage coach excursions. In recent years it has sometimes been on display at the Isle of Wight Bus and Coach museum.*

CDL 899 *Bristol K5G 56-seat open-top double deck bus. This vehicle was delivered new to Southern Vectis in July 1939 as a conventional highbridge double deck bus with Eastern Coachworks body. It was converted to an open-top bus by Southern Vectis in 1959 and became the third open-top bus to be used by the operator for service on summer coastal routes. For many years the bus, known as 'The Old Girl' was also used for special excursions and private hire work, including trips to the Derby at Epsom, where it was used as a temporary grandstand inside the race course close to the winning post. It has been part of the Southern Vectis fleet for over 75 years. This photograph was taken at the Isle of Wight Steam Railway at Havenstreet station in 2012.*

Appendix 1 – List of known and likely pre-war DL survivors

DL 33 Benz 8hp car. Built 1898. First registered 12/1903. Spent some years at the National Motor Museum, Beaulieu, Hampshire. Now with Daimler-Benz AG Museum in Germany.

DL 39 Humber 2-seater car. First registered 1/1904. Owned by Denis G Warwick (2008). Currently believed to be in the USA.

DL 74 Clement type AC4R 14hp four cylinder motor wagonette. Manufactured 1903. Owned by Johnny Thomas, Carmarthen, Wales.

DL 126 1906 Rover 6hp car. Restored in the 1980s by David Bliss. Owned by Tim Day on the Isle of Wight.

DL 259 1907 Itala Grand Prix racing car. Owned by Mrs. Edgar Thornton up to 1931. Then owned by Cheverton family. On long term loan to the National Motor Museum at Beaulieu.

DL 557 1910 Mass 22hp four cylinder tourer. Sold in running order from Northwood, IW to Ohio, USA, c.1970.

DL 793 1913 four-cylinder 25hp Talbot.

DL 821 1913 Vauxhall Model C 'Prince Henry' 25hp tourer (30/98). Owned by Mrs. Frank Cheverton from new. Restored by Bob Stay in the 1950s. Now owned by the Cheverton family and on long term loan to the National Motor Museum.

DL 837 1912 Wilkinson 8hp motorcycle combination. Registered to N.H. Cullen (2008).

DL 843 1913 Daimler landaulette 30hp. Now with Daimler-Jaguar Heritage Trust.

DL 896 1913 Triumph motorcycle. Owned by Canon S.A. Griffiths, Malton in 2008.

DL 1081 c.1912 Alldays and Onions motorcycle. Owned by Mr Case on the Isle of Wight.

DL 1222 c.1919 Ford Model T two-seater car. Originally the chassis was fitted with a commercial body. Restored and owned by Bob Stay on the Isle of Wight.

DL 1626 c.1919 Royal Enfield motorcycle. On the Isle of Wight.

DL 1696 Henderson four-cylinder, 10hp motorcycle. Probably still exists on the Island.

DL 1930 1919/1920 ABC Skootamota 125cc. Restored and owned by George Davis on the Isle of Wight. This motorcycle was manufactured at Somerton, Cowes and has been in the same family ownership since new.

DL 2098 1921 Triumph motorcycle. Owned by H. Butterfield (2008).

DL 2108 Marshall 6hp traction engine "Faithfull". Built 1909 but not registered for road use until 1921. Owned in 1921 by A. Faithfull, Barnsley Farm, Ryde. Original IW County Council metal plate no. 15 still carried at 11/4/2007. Owned and rallied for several years by Bob Stay. Currently owned by the Jenkins family on the Isle of Wight.

DL 2151 c.1918 Alldays and Onions tractor. Formerly owned and rallied for many years by the late Den Phillips on the Isle of Wight. Sold at auction to a mainland owner.

DL 2218 1921 Ford Model TT two-ton open truck. Original owner was H.P. Colenutt, Broadway Garage, Sandown. Restored and owned by Bob Stay on the Isle of Wight.

DL 2478 Unidentified 1920s motorcycle.

DL 2560 1922 Arrol-Johnston 4 cylinder 'one door' limousine. Registered new to a lady owner on the Isle of Wight. This vehicle spent many years on display at the Museum of Transport in Glasgow when it was in the ownership of the Royal Scottish Automobile Club.

DL 2610 1922 Leyland Type C1 charabanc with 26 seat body. New to G.K. Nash, Ventnor then F.J. Cheek, Chale (1941) then John Golding (1964) then Geoff Golding (1981). Long term restoration project on the Isle of Wight.

DL 2679 1921 Crossley Overland tourer.

DL 2846 1909 Wallis and Steevens traction engine "Vectis" (first registered in 1922). Rescued in derelict state by John Golding. Currently at the Milestones Museum in Basingstoke.

DL 2864 1922 Wallis and Steevens convertible road roller.

DL 2949 1919 Morris Cowley. Registration issued in 1923.

DL 2961 1903 Mackenzie motorcycle. Registration issued 1923.

DL 3059 Douglas motorcycle combination. Registration issued 4/1923. On the Isle of Wight.

DL 3085 Registration issued in April 1923. Later re-issued in 1928 for Bentley saloon car.

DL 3128 1923 Aveling and Porter road roller "Invicta". Originally owned by Ryde BC.

DL 3233 1923 Rover 8hp coupe. Originally supplied by Arthur Holmes' Garage in Cowes in July 1923. Owned and maintained in excellent running order by Colin Thomas on the Isle of Wight.

DL 3304 1923 Ford Model T van, with bodywork by Harry Margham, Newport. First registered owner was Mr. J Cassell of Shorwell. Restored and owned by Bob Stay.

DL 3609 1924 Singer 10 two-seater tourer. Restored and owned by Bob Stay.

DL 3782 1924 Aveling and Porter road roller "Energy". Registration issued December 1924.

DL3819 Austin 7 Ulster. Owned by D. Tedham, Kidderminster. Registration issued 1/1/1925. Originally this number was allocated to a Morris Commercial van. The first owner of the van was W.R. Marshall of Mottistone, Isle of Wight.

DL 4057 1924 Rudge Whitworth 350cc motorcycle. Sold at auction 13/10/12.

DL 4185 Raleigh motorcycle, possibly 350cc. Registration issued July 1925.

DL 4371 1926 Morris Cowley. Sold at auction 11/6/2011 for £11,000. Possibly formerly owned by Sir Malcolm Campbell.

DL 4405 1925 Morris Cowley tourer. Originally owned by Sir John Simeon of Swainston Manor. Owned by Bob Stay on the Isle of Wight.

DL 4751 1926 Morris Cowley. Owned by Robert E. May, Abingdon, Oxon (2008).

DL 4953 1927 Fiat car. (To be verified)

DL 5084 Reconditioned c.1919 Daimler CK running chassis purchased by Vectis Bus Company in 1927 and fitted with second-hand Dodson 26-seat bus body built in 1922. Owned by John Golding on the Isle of Wight. Long term restoration project.

DL 5244 1927 BSA 350cc solo motorcycle. Part of the Norman Ball Transport Collection, c.1990.

DL 5376 1927 Matchless 250cc motorcycle. First owned by Mr. L. Harvey of Wroxall. Restored and owned by John McConnell on the Isle of Wight.

DL 5382 1927 Raleigh Model 15 250cc motorcycle. Owned by John Gregory in 1980s.

DL 5437 1927 Morris flat nose saloon. Delivered to a Yorkshire owner by John Golding in 1970s.

DL 5478 1927 Sentinel steam lorry. Original owner Westmore (IW) Ltd., Newport. Rescued from Cowes scrapyard in 1965. Current owners live in Suffolk and display vehicle at rallies.

DL 5659 1928 Austin 16/6 Gordon Landaulette. Taunton owner.

DL 5703 Triumph 500cc motorcycle with modern replacement petrol tank.

DL 5969 1927 Austin 7 G.E. Cup model. Owned by Mr Roach in Totton. Trials car. This vehicle also has another chassis and reg. no. WL 1399.

DL 6253 1929 Ariel 500cc motorcycle. Part of the Norman Ball Transport Collection, c.1990.

DL 6543 Chevrolet LQ utility vehicle now rebodied as a box van. First registered to D. Day and Sons, Bonchurch, IW on 1/8/1929. Seen in Hampshire, 2012.

DL 6596 Raleigh motorcycle. Registration issued September 1929. Kendal owner.

DL 6623 1929 Austin 16/6 Burnham saloon. Owned by Mr Grimshaw, Coulsdon, Surrey.

DL 6972 1930 Coventry Eagle motorcycle. Fully restored in 1980s by Mr Alistair Compton, Carisbrooke, IW. Sold in auction.

DL 7202 Austin 7 Mulliner boat tail two-seater. Registration issued September 1930.

DL 7243 Austin 7 RL box saloon. Registration issued October 1930. Currently in Martinhoe, Devon.

DL 7400 BSA motorcycle combination approx. 770cc. First registered in March 1931 to IW Constabulary (Police Station, Newport).

DL 7403 Austin 7 special. Registration issued March 1931. Owned by Mr T. Shore on the Isle of Wight.

DL 7439 1931 Austin 7 RK saloon. First registered 26/3/1931. This car lost its original registration in January 1994 and became KFF 116 until June 1994. It then became SV 4933. It is still active with its current owner in Aberdeenshire.

DL 7564 1931 Reo two-ton open lorry. First registered to W. Phillips, Ventnor (Burt's Brewery). Owned by John Golding on the Isle of Wight. Vehicle should be fully restored by 2015.

DL 7634 1931 Ford Model AA dropside lorry. Original owner W. Downer, builder, Totland, IW. Owned by Geoff Golding on the Isle of Wight.

DL 7638 Aveling and Porter DX four-ton road roller. Registration issued 25/8/1931. Seen at a mainland auction.

DL 7679 1931 Austin 7 Ulster. Owned by Mr R Hanaver, Worthing.

DL 7778 1932 Austin 7. Owned by Tim Day on the Isle of Wight (unrestored).

DL 7829 Austin 7 Chummy. Registration issued 4/3/1932. Photographed at Goodwood, 2003.

DL 7841 1932 Austin 7 RN saloon. First registered 16/3/1932.

DL 7904 1932 Austin 7 RN saloon chassis. Registration issued 22/4/1932. Owned by Rick Leader on the Isle of Wight.

DL 7994 1932 Ford Model A one-ton van. Registration issued 1/7/1932. Based on the Island for many years up to 1980. Fully restored by current owner in Cheshire.

DL 8150 Austin 7 Pearl cabriolet. Owned by D. Leach, Petersfield.

DL 8444 1933 Morris 10 saloon. Currently used for private hire work on the mainland.

DL 8600 1933 Austin 7 two-seat tourer. Registration issued 22/9/1933. Owned by Rick Leader on the Isle of Wight.

DL 8648 Austin 7 special. Registration issued 17/10/1933.

DL 8666 Ford Model Y saloon. Reg. issued 28/10/1933. Sold to mainland owner in 2012. Re-registered 646 CDL many years ago.

DL 8745 Austin 7 PD tourer. Registration issued 1/1/1934.

DL 8773 1934 Ford Model Y coupe with Salmons and Sons Tickford Cairns coachwork. Restored and owned by Bob Stay on the Isle of Wight.

DL 8945 1934 Austin 7 PD tourer. Registration issued 18/4/1934 to IW Electric Light Company, Ryde.

DL 8961 1934 Austin 10hp four-door saloon. Part of the Norman Ball Transport Collection, c.1990. This car is in use on the mainland and can be seen at car shows from time to time.

DL 8969 Ford Model B hot rod V8 custom. Registration issued 20/4/1934. Seen in Manchester. May be a re-registration.

DL 8xxx Morris 8 saloon. Full restoration required. Still on the Isle of Wight.

DL 9015 1934 Dennis Ace 20-seater bus with Harrington bodywork. New to Southern Vectis in July 1934. Immaculately restored and owned by Derek Priddle in Surrey.

DL 9064 Ford Model Y saloon. Registration issued 1/6/1934. Seen in Enfield in 1999.

DL 9081 1934 Austin 7 RP box saloon. Owned by Tony Hayter on the Isle of Wight.

DL 9136 1934 Vauxhall ASX with Salmons and Sons Tickford coachwork. Owned by N. Starkey, Worcester.

DL 9347 1935 Morris. Owned by Brian Crawford in Hatfield.

DL 9674 Morris 8 tourer. Registration issued 14/5/1935. Sold unrestored on eBay 2012.

DL 9706 1935 Dennis Lancet Mk. I bus with ECW 35-seat rear entrance body. Rescued from scrap by John Golding. Long term restoration project nearing completion on the mainland.

DL 9899 Austin 10 Litchfield saloon. Reg. issued 8/1935.

DL 9939 Rolls Royce. Registration issued 12/9/1935. Sold in North Wales, 2012.

ADL 170 1936 motorcycle combination. Still active on IW.

ADL 300 1936 Morris 8 saloon. Registration issued 17/3/1936. First owned by Captain R M Lunt, St. Lawrence, IW.

ADL 380 1936 Hillman Minx saloon. Registration issued 1/5/1936. Owned by Tony Hayter on the Isle of Wight.

ADL 598 1936 Austin 10 Litchfield saloon. Supplied by Frank Cheverton, 1/7/1936. First owned by A. Marvin, Newport.

ADL 837 1936 Morris 8 tourer.

ADL 954 Lanchester saloon. Very poor condition with no

engine. Offered for sale on eBay in 2010, result unknown.

ADL 962 1937 Austin 10 van, first registered 1/1/1937. Rescued from a Wroxall builder's yard by the late John Richie. Owned and used by Colin Thomas on the Isle of Wight.

BDL 29 1937 Morris 8 saloon (to be confirmed?)

BDL 148 1937 Morris 8 tourer. Owned by Roger Price in Staffordshire.

BDL 171 1937 Royal Enfield motorcycle. Still active on the IW.

BDL 235 1937 Morris 8 tourer. Registration issued 1/5/1937. First owned by Miss. C. Firth, Godshill, IW. Hampshire owner.

BDL 279 1937 Ford Model Y saloon. Still active on the Island.

BDL 400 1937 Ford 10. Owned by Mr. Newnham on the IW.

BDL 451 Austin Cambridge saloon. Vehicle was for sale around 2009 with number sold. Current location unknown.

BDL 648 1937 Ariel motorcycle. Still active on the Isle of Wight.

BDL 887 1937 Morris 8 tourer. In use on the mainland. Location unknown.

CDL 89 1937 Morris 8 tourer. In use on the mainland. Location unknown.

CDL 437 Morris 8 van. Auctioned 11/6/2011. Stated as 1936 and supplied by Fowlers Ltd, Newport. Blue with side windows. Date doesn't match registration. IW records state 1/12/1938. For sale again in 2012, now red with no side windows but stated new full restoration. Location unknown.

CDL 461 1938 Morris 10 saloon. First owner A. Partridge, Ventnor. In use on the mainland.

CDL 707 1939 Austin Cambridge. Owned by Bill Steward on the Isle of Wight.

CDL 792 Bedford WTB coach with Duple 26-seat bodywork. Formerly Shotters Ltd. First registered on 1st June 1939. Owned by John Woodhams on the Isle of Wight.

CDL 799 1939 James motorcycle delivery van. Originally owned by Shanklin Co-operative Society store. On display at the Bentley Museum. In occasional use.

CDL 806 1939 Francis Barnett cruiser 350cc motorcycle (?).

CDL 877 1939 Morris 8 E tourer. First owner R.E. Banks, Sandown. In use on the mainland.

CDL 899 1939 Bristol K5G 56-seat open top bus. Owned and operated by Southern Vectis on the Isle of Wight since new.

CDL 920 1939 Bedford WTB coach with Duple 26-seat bodywork. Owned by Brett of Guyhirn, Isle of Ely, Cambridgeshire in 2009. Long term restoration project.

CDL 998 Ford groundsman's tractor. Built before 1939 but was probably unregistered when new. First reg'd in June 1940.

117 vehicles in total (approx. 35% on Isle of Wight, 60% on the mainland and 5% overseas).

Existence to be verified

It is thought that there are probably several more surviving pre-war DL-registered vehicles, especially motorcycles, but no further details have been traced to date.

List compiled by Colin Thomas and Mark Chessell in May 2014 with assistance from several other vintage vehicle enthusiasts.

Appendix 2 – Isle of Wight vehicle manufacturers and coachbuilders

The Isle of Wight has a rich engineering and manufacturing heritage which extends back to the mid-nineteenth century. Partly driven by natural locational advantages, its historic national importance for yachting and the availability of a skilled workforce the Island has long been a popular part of the UK for shipbuilding and the construction of small boats. Up to the Second World War, J.S. White and Co. Ltd. of Cowes was a major shipbuilder and Saunders-Roe Ltd. of Cowes and East Cowes was an important manufacturer of aircraft and flying boats. These two companies produced vessels/ aircraft for civilian and military use.

Production of road vehicles on the Island on the other hand tended to be much smaller scale and generally concentrated on meeting local needs rather than aiming to cater for a regional or national market. In the horse-drawn transport era up to around 1920 the manufacture of stage coaches, carriages, vans, agricultural vehicles, etc. was widely dispersed with a mix of medium-sized and small firms serving their immediate communities. Many family coachbuilding firms became very skilled at manufacturing a range of horse-drawn vehicles for local businesses and individuals. At the start of the twentieth century several of these firms, sensing the opportunities associated with motor vehicles, began to diversify into building bodies for cars, charabancs and lorries. Some of them possessed all the skills required to build, equip and fit bodies to a range of chassis. Others would sub-contract certain tasks (e.g. to specialist blacksmiths, upholsterers, painters and sign writers).

Kelly's Directory of the Isle of Wight for 1908 provides a fascinating insight into the range of firms which were actively engaged in the manufacture of horse-drawn and motor vehicles at that time within the following categories:-

Coach and carriage builders

John BARTLETT junior, Harrow Cottages, Nettlestone, St. Helens

Robert BULL, 149 High Street, Newport; workshop, 9 Coppins Bridge, Newport

R. Bird CHEVERTON and Co. Ltd., 50 and 51 Lugley Street, Newport and 4 Lower St. James Street, Newport

COTTON, PALMER and (Thomas) SIVELL, Albert Place, High Street, Ryde

Harry MARGHAM, 58 and 59 Crocker Street, Newport

MEARMAN's carriage factory, 35 Pyle Street, and Town Lane, Newport

G.H. MULLISS and Co., Nelson Street, Ryde

Harry George NORRIS, High Street, Freshwater

POLLARD and Sons, 17 Hill Street, Ryde

ROUT and Son, 35 South Street, Newport

Thomas Archibald EDGAR, works, York Road, Sandown

J.V. TRICKETT, Trafalgar Road, Newport

Coach painters

MARTIN Brothers, 1 and 3 Albert Street, Ventnor

Harry MIDLANE, 28 Albert Street, Newport

Coach and motor trimmer

William George SCAMMELL, 8 Anglesea Street; workshop, 1 Manor Gardens, Ryde

Motor car manufacturers

A.M. CHEVERTON (garage), 138 and 139 High Street and 23 Quay Street, Newport

R. Bird CHEVERTON and Co. Ltd., 51 Lugley Street, Newport

CLARK and BLACHFORD, 58 High Street, Cowes

Ernest du BOWLAY, 96 High Street, Cowes

Motor engineers

T.B. BRIGGS, Arctic Road, Cowes

R. Bird CHEVERTON and Co. Ltd., 50 and 51 Lugley Street, Newport

T. and E.W. JENKINS, 49 Upper St. James Street, and works, Orchard Street, Newport

J.G. and W. JOLLIFFE, Bonchurch

Edmund WARD and Co., 10 Monkton Street, Ryde

Motor car engineer

Augustus Charles CLARK, 4A George Street, Ryde and Bembridge

Further research is required to determine the scale of the motor vehicle manufacturing of the above firms. Many of the coach and carriage manufacturers probably never switched to producing motor cars and some of the motor car manufacturers and engineers may only have traded for a few years. The remainder of this appendix contains brief notes on the activities of the Isle of Wight firms who are known to have produced motor vehicles before the Second World War.

Liquid Fuel Engineering Company, East Cowes

Liquid Fuel Engineering Company (LIFU) was founded by Henry Alonso House, a distinguished American inventor. Mr House developed and patented a revolutionary steam engine which was powered by a paraffin burner rather than conventional coal. This had significant operational, space saving and economic advantages. Initially the company was based at Teddington on Thames and the engines were used to power launches. In 1894, supported by a major investment by financier Robert Rintoul Symon, LIFU relocated to the site of the Columbine shed in East Cowes. This was probably because Cowes, in the latter years of Queen Victoria's reign, was seen as the ideal place for the promotion of the company's launches to wealthy people who raced their yachts in the annual regatta.

Anticipating a large increase in demand for steam-powered road vehicles Henry House and his son Henry House junior decided to diversify the company. Within twelve months they had designed and developed some experimental vehicles and these went into production around 1896. A fairly standard chassis formed the basis of a variety of vans, lorries, charabancs and cars. Please refer to chapter 1 for several photographs of LIFU vehicles. Virtually all of the components were manufactured in East Cowes and assembled to meet the specific requirements of customers from around the country and overseas. In the late 1890s the company was widely considered to be one of the most successful manufacturers of steam-powered road vehicles in England.

Following the death of Mr. Symon, however, his executors decided that LIFU's factory at East Cowes (which had employed around 220 skilled workers) should be closed. They insisted that "every last bolt and plank of wood at the site should be sold". Thus the company, which had real potential for expansion, was dealt a shattering blow. LIFU continued to exist for a few more years at Poole and then Southampton, partly by contracting other firms to build their more advanced lighter steam-powered cars. Sadly, however, LIFU ceased trading around 1910 and the company which had promised so much was able to deliver relatively little commercial success.

Arthur Creeth, Nettlestone

Arthur Herbert Creeth was born in 1845 in Brighstone, where his father William was the village blacksmith. He took a keen interest in his father's business and learned many horse-shoeing, wrought iron and bicycle repair skills in the family smithy. In 1865 together with his brother Henry he built a quadcycle with rubber tyres, a very advanced machine at that time. He then worked as a smith for the London and South Western Railway in Nine Elms, Lambeth for several years. After returning to the Isle of Wight Arthur Creeth purchased his own blacksmith's business in Nettlestone, near Seaview in 1873. ("Steam Dreams: The story of an Isle of Wight family called Creeth" by Lilian Creeth, published by author, 1991).

Throughout his adult life Arthur Creeth had a real passion for steam-powered road transport. Around 1903 he succeeded in building a three-wheeled steam-powered English Mechanic car in his smithy workshop (see photograph in chapter 1). In March 1909 he fulfilled a long-term ambition and started operating a local bus service between Ryde and Seaview using steam-powered charabancs and buses. Three of his early vehicles were a 1908 Gardner-Serpollet charabanc (DL 299), a 1910 Darracq-Serpollet bus DL 502 and a second-hand Clarkson-National bus (DL 1614). The Creeth family continued to operate this local bus service under the name of "Premier Motor Service" until 1930, utilising steam-powered vehicles until 1922. Arthur Creeth and his colleagues built charabanc, bus and lorry bodies for several of their own steam-powered vehicles (including an open-top double

deck body for DL 1614) and are known to have built at least one large charabanc body for a petrol-engined Dennis in 1919 (see photograph of DL 1463 in chapter 3).

Witham Brothers, Pyle Street, Newport

The above photograph shows the premises of Witham Brothers Motor Engineers, probably around 1920. Relatively little is known about this Isle of Wight company, apart from the fact that it was already in existence by 1885 for the manufacture of invalid carriages. From the image it appears that over twenty staff were employed. The Isle of Wight firm is known to have specialised in the manufacture of wheelchairs, carriages and equipment for people with mobility difficulties and may also have been involved in the manufacture of bicycles and motorcycles. Owner James Witham was a keen pioneer motorcyclist and a photograph exists of him riding his Douglas motorcycle registered DL 1157.

Chevertons of Newport

The Frank Cheverton Ltd. company history "A Century of Progress: 1852 to 1952" records that William Cheverton, a cabinet maker, started in business as a coach builder and repairer at Broadlands, Newport in 1852. William Cheverton took his younger son, Richard Bird Cheverton, into the firm which prospered and soon moved to 34 Lugley Street. Further expansion required more space and adjoining premises were purchased when they became available. Following this growth the firm was catering for coach building, repairing, painting and harness making. A Cycle Department was also added. In 1872 William Cheverton died and the business was carried on by his two sons, with Richard Bird Cheverton as manager.

Chevertons became well known for their carriages, which though stronger, were much lighter in construction than other makes. This came to the notice of Queen Victoria's Master-of-the-Horse and orders were received from Her Majesty. She purchased 17 Chevertons' carriages in total and following the Queen's patronage many orders were received from across the country. In addition the Queen placed some further orders for snow sleighs, bathing carriages and barouches, built to her special instructions, to be sent as presents to many Royal Households abroad.

By the end of the nineteenth century R. Bird Cheverton had six sons engaged in the family business. In 1897 one of these sons, Frank Arthur Cheverton, started work in the Cycle Department. A year or so later Frank went to the Smith's Shop and afterwards to the Fitting Shop. In 1900 he was employed by the Progress Motor Company in Coventry for three years. He then went on to gain further technical and sales experience in one of the largest motor garages on the mainland. The first work undertaken by Chevertons on motor vehicles was in 1899 – 1900 when they trimmed the car bodies and bound wheels for LIFU steam-powered cars and lorries which were being manufactured at East Cowes.

In 1905 Frank Cheverton returned to the Isle of Wight and opened a Motor Department in Lugley Street. There were very few motor cars on the Island at that time but the repair side of the business increased swiftly and car and tyre agencies were taken up. Most spare parts had to be made in the Smith's Shops and special bodies for the chassis were made in the Body Shop. In 1910 a new Motor Repair Shop was built and fitted with the latest equipment. The Ford dealership for the Island was signed in 1914 and this was followed by the Fordson Tractor dealership in 1919. Unfortunately it is not known how many car and commercial vehicle bodies were built and fitted by Chevertons but they must have produced a large number in the period up to 1939, especially on Ford chassis.

Mr. R. Bird Cheverton sold the business in 1923. His son Frank purchased the Ford Car and Tractor Departments and approximately one third of the premises. In 1927 Frank Cheverton purchased the remaining two thirds of the original premises in Lugley Street and once again catered for all makes of vehicles, taking on the Austin dealership in 1930. In 1933 Frank Cheverton Ltd. was formed as a private limited company. The business focused on the sale and repair of Ford, Fordson and Austin vehicles and was also involved in the manufacture of some special bodies and car hire up to the Second World War.

George H. Mulliss and Company, Nelson Street, Ryde

This was a long-established coach and carriage building business in Ryde which is understood to have carried on trading up to the 1950s. Information about the company's motor vehicle body construction and repair work is limited but it is known that Mullis was awarded and completed one major contract in 1906. This was for the construction of seven 30-seat semi-enclosed charabanc bodies for the Isle of Wight Express Motor Syndicate Ltd. These were built for the new Milnes-Daimler 28/30hp vehicles which were bought to replace the 24hp double-deck Milnes-Daimlers which had been found to be under-powered for the Island's hilly roads in 1905. The seven bodies are believed to have been built and fitted by Mulliss to new Milnes-Daimler chassis between January and July 1906. The charabancs were registered as DL 129, DL 130, and DL 133 to 137. (see picture of DL 130 in chapter 2).

Harry Margham and Sons, Crocker Street, Newport

This major coachbuilding and bodywork repairs business was established by Harry Margham in 1888, a few years after he moved to the Isle of Wight from Southampton. Initially Harry Margham traded as a coachbuilder and wheelwright of horse-drawn vehicles at 59 Crocker Street, Newport. In 1902 Harry built a new car body for a steam-powered car, make unknown. From that date up to the Second World War the firm was very active in building and repairing bodies for a wide variety of horse-drawn and motor vehicles.

During 1911 Harry built his first van body on a Napier chassis and this was followed by other commercial vehicles for local businesses. The firm changed its name to Harry Margham and Sons after two of Harry's sons joined the business. In 1921 the company built their first open charabanc body. During the 1920s and 1930s Marghams built and repaired many bodies for lorries, charabancs, buses and coaches for a large number of Isle of Wight businesses. The firm developed an excellent reputation for its attractive and well-engineered bodywork. For further information and photographs relating to Harry Margham and Sons, especially their buses and coaches, please refer to the author's previous book "Independent Bus Services on the Isle of Wight" (Chine Publishing, 2012).

Frank Sivell, Ventnor

In the early 1920s Frank Sivell is known to have built several charabanc bodies in Ventnor. One example of his work from around 1922 is the Oldsmobile charabanc DL 2763 owned by Crinage of Ventnor, a large photograph of which is contained in chapter 3. Mr. Sivell was clearly a very skilful coachbuilder although his designs were somewhat plain in appearance.

Gilbert Campling Ltd., Somerton, Cowes

Immediately after the First World War the firm of Gilbert Campling Ltd. negotiated the production, marketing and distribution rights for the ABC Skootamota. This was an early motor scooter, powered by a 125cc engine, which had been designed by the prolific inventor Granville Bradshaw. The All British Company Ltd. (ABC) had been formed in 1911 by Walter Adams, Granville Bradshaw and Ronald Charteris for the development and production of engines for aeroplanes, motor cycles and cars.

According to Barry M. Jones' book "Granville Bradshaw: a flawed genius?" (Panther Publishing Ltd., 2008) the first Skootamotas were made at the ABC Works in Hersham during early 1919. Production models, with 16" rims, were produced from July by Gilbert Campling possibly at Selsdon Aero and Engineering Company Ltd. of 28 Sanderstead Road, Croydon before moving to the vacant Somerton Works, Cowes. These were almost certainly in the former aeroplane workshops on Somerton airfield, established in 1916 by John Samuel White and Co. Ltd. for assembling aeroplanes for the Great War until their production ceased in January 1919, making the workshops vacant by June 1919. Gilbert Campling put Gilbert Campling Ltd. into voluntary liquidation in November 1920. Skootamota production appears to have ceased in late 1920 or early 1921 soon after which J.S. White and Co. Ltd. sold the Somerton airfield and works to S.E. Saunders Ltd. for aircraft production. It is believed that around 3,200 Skootamotas were sold by 1922, of which around 100 still exist.

Harry Midlane, 28 Albert Street, Newport

Harry Midlane owned a long-established firm of coach painters in Newport. He is believed to have specialised in vehicle painting and sign writing but may also have been responsible for building bodies for a small number of motor vehicles. Very little is known about Harry Midlane's business but he was certainly active from 1908 until 1927 when he was involved in building and fitting a small charabanc body to an Oldsmobile chassis. This vehicle was first registered as DL 5039 around March 1927.

Appendix 3 – Non-DL Isle of Wight vehicles up to 1939

In the early years of motoring from 1904 to 1921 it is estimated that approximately 90% of 'resident' Isle of Wight motor vehicles carried "DL" registrations. The Isle of Wight County Council and many other vehicle registration authorities preferred to have locally owned vehicles with locally distinctive number plates. It was often the case that "DL" registration numbers were returned to the County Council to be re-issued to other vehicles if the original vehicles moved to or were sold to new owners on the mainland. A good example of this practice is the sale of Isle of Wight Express Motor Syndicate's initial fleet of nine Milnes-Daimler double deck buses to a London operator in October 1905. The original numbers DL 75 to DL 81 (inclusive), DL 109 and DL 110 were returned and the vehicles were subsequently allocated London registration numbers in the "LC" series. This procedure also sometimes happened in reverse with some second-hand mainland-registered vehicles being issued with "DL" registration numbers when they were 'imported' by Isle of Wight businesses or individuals.

These official vehicle registration changes did not always take place, however. Some manufacturers (e.g. the Scottish company Argyll) had a general policy of registering their new vehicles with number plates local to their factories (SB in the case of Argyll) and these were normally left unchanged when delivered to their new owners around the country.

The following photographs show some non-DL Isle of Wight cars and buses which were built before the Second World War. They were always in the minority but nevertheless formed an important part of the overall 'stock' of motor vehicles on the Island. Most local firms and residents preferred to have an Isle of Wight "DL" registration number on their commercial or domestic vehicles but some people were willing to purchase good quality second-hand vehicles with mainland registrations if the opportunity arose. An example of this policy is provided by Wavell's Enterprise Bus Service which purchased a mixture of new and second-hand Isle of Wight and mainland-registered buses between 1921 and 1939.

Immediately after the Second World War the Isle of Wight economy experienced a strong recovery as thousands of British families returned to the Island for their summer seaside holidays. Car, commercial vehicle and bus manufacturers took a couple of years to get geared up for major production of new vehicles and this meant that some Isle of Wight businesses purchased second-hand pre-war vehicles from the mainland in order to meet the needs of their customers. A major example of this practice involved Southern Vectis buying several buses and coaches from Cardiff Corporation, Hants and Dorset and the City of Oxford Motor Services Ltd. to supplement its existing fleet. Typically these elderly vehicles worked for a further five to ten years on the Island before being replaced by new DL-registered buses and coaches.

AN 258 *Mors 12hp four-cylinder tonneau, c.1902. This is thought to be one of the earliest motor vehicles on the Isle of Wight. Owned by John Bailey, a draper in Shanklin, the Belgian car was driven from London to the Isle of Wight by his son Harry, aged 18. This photo was taken at Hale Common (between Arreton and Apse Heath) probably in the second half of 1904, soon after it became a legal requirement for motor vehicles to carry number plates. AN 258 was registered in mid-1904 by the former West Ham County Borough Council. Harry Bailey and his brother Gilbert ran a taxi and car maintenance business in Shanklin for around fifteen years until they were forced to cease trading by the austere trading conditions during the First World War.*

A.N258

Princess Beatrice driving a Daimler car, c.1904. *Although only part of this vehicle is visible in the photograph it has been positively identified as a royal Daimler 22hp car dating from around 1903. Princess Beatrice (1857 – 1944) was the youngest daughter and long-term companion of Queen Victoria. She was appointed to the role of Governor of the Isle of Wight by her mother in 1896 following the untimely death of her husband, Prince Henry of Battenberg. It is not known if this photograph was taken on the Isle of Wight but Princess Beatrice spent most of her time in London or on the Isle of Wight. Up to 1912 her Island residence was Osborne Cottage (next door to Osborne House) and she then moved to the Governor's House at Carisbrooke Castle. Like her brother King Edward VII, Princess Beatrice was a keen early motorist. She is seen in this informal postcard picture with two of her children. Princess Ena went on to marry King Alfonso XIII of Spain in 1906 when she was eighteen years old.*

John Lee White's 7/9hp Vauxhall car with phaeton seat. *John Lee White, the son of famous Cowes shipbuilder J.S. White, was one of the earliest car owners on the Isle of Wight. He lived at Seafield House, Pelham Fields, Ryde from 1898 to 1912 and was a committee member of the Isle of Wight Motorists' Association in 1905. Mr. White is known to have ordered this vehicle (which exists to this day) on 19th March 1905 and owned it from new. It was manufactured in Lambeth and has a body made by Abraham Meier of Redhill, Surrey. Unfortunately the original registration number of this car is unknown. It currently carries the number plate A 317 which is believed to have been obtained when the vehicle was restored in the 1960s. Prior to that the Vauxhall carried the Surrey registration number P 8921 which may have been allocated to it when Mr. White moved to the mainland in 1912/1913. It has not so far been possible to discover whether the car originally had a low "DL" registration number. Be that as it may, this beautiful little survivor definitely qualifies to appear in this book.*

Miss Benest's 24/40hp Fiat tourer. *Contained within Cleone de Heveningham Benest's personal scrapbook was this fine photograph of the young woman at the wheel of her large Fiat car. Miss Benest lived at Ryde throughout the Edwardian period and this picture was probably taken around 1910. The Fiat carries a London registration number. As well as using the vehicle to meet her varied travel needs on the Island and mainland Miss Benest drove the car in a number of competitive hill trials, achieving excellent results. The car was equipped with a striking boa constrictor horn which produced a very loud and deep warning sound when required.*

OS 41 – Steam-powered bus operated by Arthur Creeth of Nettlestone, c.1910. *In 1909 Arthur Creeth, an established blacksmith, started operating a regular bus service between Ryde and Seaview which his family would continue to run until 1930 (trading as Premier Motor Service). From 1909 to 1922 most of the vehicles in the fleet were steam-powered and the vehicle bodies were often built by Mr Creeth in his workshop. This photograph shows a Darracq-Serpollet steam-powered vehicle with a 28-seat charabanc body built at Nettlestone. The photograph is believed to have been taken around 1912.*

SB 221 Argyll 10/12hp two-seater, painted green and first registered in April 1911. *This lovely sharp photograph shows an attractive little Argyll car in Union Street, Ryde. The vehicle is parked outside the former Wilts and Dorset Bank and the picture was probably taken around 1912. In 1916 official records show that this vehicle was registered to a Mr. D Cameron of Bedford Place, London. Argyll cars were made in Alexandria in Dunbartonshire but the company chose to register many of them with Argyllshire (SB) plates regardless of where the owner lived. This was a kind of free advertising.*

"Granny's first car" – Napier CR 1439, first registered in Southampton in 1912. *This photo was taken at the junction of Pier Street and Albert Street in Ventnor, outside Brown's Coaching Establishment. The note on the back of the original photograph is believed to refer to Mrs. M. Brown, one of the owners of this long-established family firm which provided a range of horse-drawn transport services in and around the town. Although undated the photo appears to have been taken before the First World War. The large Napier car probably earned its keep by driving small parties of affluent summer visitors to see popular tourist attractions such as Carisbrooke Castle and Godshill. Around the mid-1930s the business was sold to Mr. G K Nash and he developed Brown's premises in Pier Street as a coach station for his round-the-Island tours and excursions. Nash continued to operate the Ventnor town bus service linking the two railway stations with all parts of the seaside town. He retained the previous fleetname "Brown's Bus" until he sold his bus and coach operations to Southern Vectis in 1956.*

Recruitment of volunteer soldiers at Ryde Esplanade, c.1914. *A large crowd gathered outside the entrance to Ryde Pier to hear some speeches encouraging young men to join the British army for the First World War. The car nearest to the photographer was a Lorraine Dietrich with London registration number LA 7196. This 18/20hp vehicle was built around 1911. The car immediately behind is probably another Lorraine Dietrich, a later model, perhaps a 1914 20/30hp open drive limousine or landaulette. Finally the third car in front of the W H Smith and Son newsagents' shop is believed to be a Talbot of around 1913/1914.*

Fleet of steam wagons at Pan Roller Mill, Newport. *In the period up to around 1930 steam wagons were very important for hauling heavy loads on the Isle of Wight. The date of this photograph is unknown but it shows an impressive line-up of five such vehicles and their two-man crews which would have been used for transporting grain and flour around the Island. The vehicles are probably Foden overtypes and most likely would have carried "M", "MA" or "MB" Cheshire number plates. Foden's factory was in Sandbach and the company had a policy to register their new vehicles locally. The vehicles were owned by Thomas, Gater, Bradfield and Company Ltd., a firm of flour millers who owned the large Pan Roller Mill in the early 1920s. Pan Mill was the largest mill on the Island. The nineteenth century mill building still exists as part of the present Mill Court Business Centre.*

Royal Rolls Royce carrying the Prince of Wales on a visit to the Isle of Wight, 1926. *On 22nd July 1926 the Prince of Wales (and future King Edward VIII) made an official visit to the Isle of Wight. He is seen here arriving at Ryde Town Hall met by a cheering crowd. The Royal car is a new Rolls Royce Phantom Mk 1, c.1926, registration number YO 6111. It was being driven by William Ayers who was a chauffeur for the Royal Family for many years. According to the late Mr. Ayers' granddaughter, Mrs. Sarah Locke, this fine vehicle still exists and is located in Germany.*

Standard Fordson tractor at Bathingbourne Farm, near Newchurch, 29th April 1930. *This is an early Fordson Model N tractor, c.1922 which was built in Cork, Eire. It was being driven by Will Ford, very close to the site of the present day annual Garlic Festival. The tractor was fitted with a water air wash and iron cleats on the rear wheels. It is unusual in that it does not show a stack pipe or high air intake, most likely to enable it to access low farm buildings. Iron wheels were common at this time, especially on stony land, as the old tyres punctured easily. By the mid-1930s most tractors were fitted with rubber tyres but this reverted to iron wheels with cleats or spade lugs in 1942 when rubber was in short supply. Many tractors were not road licensed before the Second World War if the farm was all in one block away from the road or if the vehicle was driven on roads between fields for less than six miles per week. Such tractors did not need to have registration numbers. Registered tractors normally had their DL numbers painted on the back of one of the rear mudguards and on the radiator blind at the front. This tractor does not have a blind fitted so it might still have had a number as the blind had been removed. In all likelihood this tractor would have worked the land at Bathingbourne Farm for many years and would have been one of a large number of Fordson vehicles on the Isle of Wight before the war. These tractors were all supplied and serviced by Frank Cheverton Ltd. in Newport, the only Fordson dealer on the Island.*

Horse-drawn hoe at Bathingbourne Farm, 29th July 1930. *Exactly three months later the photograph on the right was also taken at Bathingbourne Farm. It is included in the book to demonstrate that tractors and horses were both in active use on Isle of Wight farms for different tasks between the wars. According to the information on the rear of the original photo the horse is being led by Frank Draper. At the rear Bert Morris is steering the hoe which would weed between rows of crops. In the centre a group of five Irish farm labourers are seen holding individual hoes. They would have been responsible for removing weeds around specific plants which had been missed by the horse drawn hoe. Seven men were required for this strenuous manual work which today would be carried out by a single man or woman and a tractor pulling a crop sprayer.*

OV 8100 Dennis Lancet Mk 1 32-seat coach, built in 1932. *This solid and reliable pre-war vehicle, with Auto Cellulose bodywork, was purchased by Southern Vectis from City of Oxford Motor Services Ltd. in 1945. The coach was a valuable member of the company's fleet of buses and coaches until it was withdrawn in 1950.*

References

Benest, Miss Cleone de Heveningham, *original personal scrapbook (1905 to 1911)*

Chessell, Mark P., *Independent Bus Services on the Isle of Wight,* Chine Publishing, 2012

Couling, David, *An Isle of Wight Camera 1914 to 1945,* Dovecote Press, Dorset, 1982

Creeth, Lilian, *Steam Dreams: the story of an Isle of Wight family called Creeth,* published by author, 1991

East Cowes Heritage Centre, *LIFU, East Cowes, 1894 – 1900,* published in 2008

Frank Cheverton Ltd., Newport, Isle of Wight, *A Century of Progress 1852 – 1952,* 1952

Goodman, Bryan, *Motoring around Surrey,* Tempus Publishing, 2001. Reprinted by the History Press, Stroud, Gloucestershire, 2013

Hall, Patrick, *The motor bus in the Isle of Wight before 1919,* published by author, 2012

Isle of Wight County Press, various issues of this weekly local newspaper from 1900 to 2014

Isle of Wight Record Office, o*riginal Isle of Wight County Council DL-registration ledgers,* covering the period November 1926 to September 1939

Jones, Barry M., *Granville Bradshaw: a flawed genius?,* Panther Publishing Ltd., 2008

Newman, Richard, *Southern Vectis: the first sixty years,* published by Ensign Publications, Southampton for Southern Vectis, 1989

Nicholson, T.R., *Passenger Cars 1863 – 1904,* Blandford Press Ltd., 1970

Nicholson, T.R., *Passenger Cars 1905 – 1912,* Blandford Press Ltd., 1971

Scott-Moncrieff, David, *Veteran and Edwardian motor cars,* B.T. Batsford, Ltd., London, second impression, 1956

Sprake, Derek, *Put out the flag: the story of Isle of Wight carriers 1860 – 1960,* Cross Publishing, 1993

Vauxhall Motors Ltd., *Veteran, Vintage and Historic Vauxhalls 1903 – 1938,* c.1970

Vincent, Don and Roberts, Chris, *Isle of Wight Registrations in the original DL-series, DL 1 to DL 9999 (1903 to 1935), second edition 2008 with 2010 supplement*

Woodall, Noel and Heaton, Brian, *Car Numbers then and now*, Registrations Publications, 2008

List of Photographers

The late Cleone de Heveningham Benest collection: 16, 26 (lower), 135 (upper)
The late Fay Brown collection: 29, 43 (DL 1463), 74 (upper and lower)
Carisbrooke Castle Museum Trustees: 31, 47, 135 (lower), 136, 138
Mark Chessell: 1, 84/85, 94, 95 (2 images), 96, 104, 105, 106 (4 images), 107, 108, 114, 116, 120, rear cover
Alan Cross: 71, 72 (lower), 76 (upper), 81 (lower), 142
Alan Cross / J.F. Higham collection: 70, 82
Jeanette Davis collection: 95 (upper left)
Mark Earp collection: 14, 132
Richard Flack collection: 23 (upper and lower)
Nigel Flux collection: 54
Keir Foss collection: 37 (DL 1338), 43 (DL 1474), 49 (lower), 50 (upper and lower), 62 (left), 65 (upper)
Shelagh Gaylard collection: 61
John Golding collection: 27 (upper), 35, 37 (DL 1353), 44, 57 (DL 3570), 64, 88 (upper and lower), 89, 139
Geoff Golding collection: 34, 51 (lower), 100, 101, 110 (lower), 111
Bryan Goodman collection: 8 (3 images), 9
John Gregory collection: 36 (upper), 43 (DL 1560), 46, 80 (right), 81 (upper)
Patrick Hall collection: 28, 53, 55
Patrick Hall collection – courtesy of the late Mr. Kenneth Guy: 36
Patrick Hall collection – courtesy of Mrs. M.E. Harwood: 51
Tim Harding collection: front cover, 19, 20, 21 (upper and lower), 25, 39, 45, 49 (upper), 52, 58, 69 (lower), 73
Isle of Wight Record Office: 18, 53 (DL 3134)
Alan Lambert collection: 26 (upper)
Sarah Locke collection: 32, 140
John McConnell: 109
Laurence Mortram collection: 63
Omnibus Society: 79
Barry Price collection: 38, 53 (DL 3088), 57 (DL 3707), 59, 68, 128
Peter Relf: 83, 113 (upper)
Tim Sargeant collection: 24 (upper), 134
Janice Smith collection: 112
Bob Stay collection: 97, 113 (lower)
Colin Thomas: 90, 91, 92, 93, 102, 103 (lower), 115, 118
Colin Thomas collection: 30 (lower), 72 (upper), 80 (left), 98, 99, 103 (upper), 110 (upper), 117
Ventnor and District Local History Society: 11, 17, 33 (upper and lower), 56, 77, 137
Don Vincent: 6, 119
Roger Warwick collection: 48

All other photographs are from the author's collection